MW01617960

Luminosity

LUMINOSITY

The Paintings of Stephen Hannock

Preface by **S. Lane Faison, Jr.**

Introduction by **Duncan Christy**

CHRONICLE BOOKS
SAN FRANCISCO

DEDICATION

Printed in Hong Kong

Library of Congress Cataloging-in-Publication Data available.

ISBN: 0-8118-2832-8 (hc)

Book design: Amy Henderson
Art photographs: Hiro Ihara, Stephen Petegorsky, Gamma One Conversions, Wolfgang Freithof

Distributed in Canada by Raincoast Books, 8680 Cambie Street, Vancouver BC V6P 6M9

10 9 8 7 6 5 4 3 2 1

Chronicle Books
85 Second Street
San Francisco, CA 94105

www.chroniclebooks.com

Love and appreciation to the following folks for the adventures and support that make the art come to life.

Marshall, Liz, Sal and Bridget, Bette and Agnes Mongan, Leonard Baskin, Daniel Hodermarsky, Maurice Berger, Duncan Christy, Hugh M. Davies, Suzannah Fabing, Lane and Jody Faison, Hal Fischer, Robert Atkins, Ashton Hawkins, Irene Hunter, Louis Bacon, John and Gretchen Berggruen, Tom and Meredith Brokaw, Anne Crawford, James F. Dicke II, Robin and Julie Graham, Gil and Lucy Lamphere, William and Karen Lauder, Meredith and Cornelia Long, Valerie McKenzie, Liz Mayer, Stacey Winston and Christine Wachter, Tom McNamee, Louise McNamee, Barbara Novak and Brian O'Doherty, Graham Nash and R. Mac Holbert, Michael and Pat Peyser, Maureen Regan, Mimi Rogers, Michelle Rosenberg, Steve and Jamie Tisch, Sting and Trudie Styler, Wheelock Whitney, Cows and the Willard Clan.

—Stephen Hannock

New York

CONTENTS

PREFACE

In what was undoubtedly a message to critics, Mark Rothko said a work of art is not *about* an experience; it *is* an experience. Applied to painting, this has to mean a *visual* experience, a response to *visual* forms, elements of a *visual* language. Whatever is merely *visible* can be absorbed by looking, but to reach the visual you must see; that is, perceive, comprehend.

Such is the case with Stephen Hannock. The foregoing thoughts are offered as a way to set the stage for a give-and-take (it might be called a transaction) between artist and viewer about the visual terms of Hannock's art.

His special concern is light—light as something all-consuming, even when the painting's subject happens to be, for example, a view of the great oxbow in the Connecticut River near Northampton, Massachusetts. Technically and aesthetically, Hannock bathes Thomas Cole's famous vision of the scene in a new, lowered light, which he explores *visually* in tones of varying hue, intensity, and value. Then comes his special refinement: After the oil surface has dried, he carefully burnishes it, trapping, ever so subtly, the "actual" light outside the picture itself. There is a soft, secret glow.

As with all Hannocks, that glow suffuses the landscape forms. Landscape is not exactly the vogue in painting, but Stephen Hannock, with his special technique and gifts, has mastered this traditional form and invested it with modernity. You can *look* at his paintings for a long time with an unalloyed pleasure. But you can also *see* them, if you're willing to be charmed and provoked by the painter's distinctive visual language. And, as with the finest works of art, they will require you to think about them and be affected by them—to serve you as reference for the other art that you know—long after you have turned away from the individual frames.

Claude Lorrain and J. M. W. Turner, come welcome a new disciple!

—S. Lane Faison, Jr.

Williamstown, Massachusetts

AN EXCUSE TO MAKE A LIGHTSCAPE

Anyone who thinks that paintings are delicate objects—and that creating them is akin to microsurgery—should observe Stephen Hannock in his Soho studio.

Clad in spattered shorts, a T-shirt, and running shoes, with jazz music throbbing soulfully behind him, Hannock is putting the finishing touches on another of his "incendiary nocturnes." A canvas approximately five feet by three, this one is entitled *Mauve Dusk* [plate 57], its title a direct homage to the nineteenth-century landscapist George Inness. The trademark touches of Hannock's landscapes—or, as he likes to call them, "lightscapes"—are here: a foreground of gray-green water reflecting a sky precisely the same color; an intermediate band of dull gray-brown riverbank from which bare, brushlike trees hollowly emerge; near the top an eruption of fiery light, the firework that gives the "incendiary" touch to the painting's otherwise "nocturne"-like character.

It is a moment suspended in time, a mood, that draws the eye steadily upward to the placement of the nova, then allows it to retreat to survey the whole. Brilliantly worked, its rhythms carefully controlled, this painting should fetch $40,000 at the artist's forthcoming show in Seattle; it will most likely be promised to one of his eager collectors even before the show opens. At the moment, though, Hannock has just poured water all over it, and is preparing to take an orbital sander with 220-grit wet-dry sandpaper to its surface.

This isn't a prescription for disaster, nor is the artist simply undoing something that he wishes to retouch. Polishing away happily, sending paint, resin, and water in all directions, working the surface more like a janitor than a painter, Hannock is simply utilizing the process that gives his paintings the quality that makes them unique: their extraordinary rendering of light, their "luminosity."

At forty-nine, the youthful Hannock stands at the first zenith of a career that promises to enshrine him as securely among major American painters as the nineteenth-century landscapists to whom he is frequently compared:

Thomas Cole, Frederic Edwin Church, Sanford Robinson Gifford, and their gifted brethren. Producing some seventy-five paintings a year, he is collected widely and by a list studded with celebrities from the worlds of culture, finance, and media. Providentially, he missed being lionized in the 1980s, at the time to his chagrin. He is therefore unscathed by the tarnished reputations that trail many of the artist-celebrities of that era, much of their work now mocked. Instead, Stephen Hannock is free to continue to grow in all the directions that he chooses. And if the Academy Award he shared last year for his technical work on the movie *What Dreams May Come* is any symbol, grow he will.

When, as a handsome adolescent, a masked Stephen Hannock crouched in a hockey goal, he could scarcely have foreseen the career that was to come. "Eating rubber" was what he did, and what he expected to do, defying pucks at higher and higher levels of play. But, in a career that has seen the potent intervention of a few key patrons and mentors, a teacher at Deerfield Academy in Massachusetts saw what Hannock could do on a sketch pad away from the rink. A brilliant artist himself, Dan Hodermarsky showed Hannock, basically, that art was cool, deep, true. That being an artist and getting the girls was not only no contradiction, but actually an enhancement.

Hockey's loss was art's gain. At Smith College, where he had migrated after a stint at Bowdoin, Hannock apprenticed with world-renowned artist Leonard Baskin. He describes the time as "the ultimate art school," and he worked aggressively in woodcuts, sculpture, anatomical drawing, and painting to give himself the formal training he lacked. Raised in middle-class circumstances, Hannock plunged into a workmanlike poverty after graduation in 1976, determined to be a painter. A beloved patron, Irene Hunter, "Mrs. H.," provided a monthly stipend that allowed him to live and work—just. Today, he draws laughs from the school audiences he occasionally addresses when he describes his post-graduate living situation: an abandoned factory in Northampton, Massachusetts. He was sharing it, and not happily, with a family of raccoons, and he had to fashion a series of ceiling-level aqueducts "to channel their piss into corner mayonnaise jars."

He was fascinated by light, and the methods of rendering it. First, it was with the Day-Glo paints that had been used in 1960s-era rock posters and that required a black light to bring out their garish intensity. Then it was phosphorescent paint, which still required the external black light unit to come to coolly meditative life but spared viewers the completely lightless rooms they would otherwise have groped around in. (Imagine the type of well-heeled crowd that attends leading art openings today wandering around in such circumstances, spilling white wine all over each other, throwing themselves out of adjustment.) His compositions were imaginary landscapes, large scale, that observers compared broadly to the imagery of pop sorcery, science fiction, and heavy metal. Hannock's own summation of them is more learned: "somewhere between Disney and Caspar David Friedrich," the nineteenth-century German Romantic painter, who, then as now, was a personal hero.

"I was always painting with oil paint," Hannock says, "but I was unable to find a voice that could yield this light, this illusion of light that phosphorescent paint could. Globs of oil paint are stunning and can be handled in magnificent ways, but they just weren't the ways I was interested in." He sensed, though, that he would have to master oil if he wanted to succeed. "I longed to express these ideas I had in a conventional medium. I want to speak in a language that most people understand."

The turning point of his career, and its key act of providence, came in 1983. "I did a painting of Northampton, Massachusetts," he recalls, "called *New England City (Northampton, Massachusetts)* [plate 1]. The light was stunning—and completely ruined by the streaks of glare that came through the sky as a result of my brush strokes and the resin I was using to quick-dry it. In frustration, I took rough-grit sandpaper and sanded the whole thing down, sanded the sky right back down to the canvas in order to start over again. And at that point, it was clear that the painting was finished. By reducing the surface of the applied paint, I had eliminated all the glare and thus was left with that pure reflection of light that I was looking for without interference."

"That pure reflection of light . . ." has been the quest of Hannock's career, and certainly of its last two decades. Once he had discovered how to achieve it, the task became how to refine and control it. He would work simultaneously in both phosphorescent and oil for a decade longer, metamorphosing as circumstances permitted. His last showing of a phosphorescent painting came in 1990 at the Tibor de Nagy Gallery in New York, where one canvas hung alongside seven new oils. Coincidentally, he was then being featured in an MTV special about hip contemporary painters that spotlighted his phosphorescent work; the television audiences had no idea that the artist was giving up that medium even as they watched.

In 1981 Hannock was a visiting artist at Harvard's Carpenter Center for the Visual Arts in Cambridge, a prestigious appointment. He had already been the youngest artist ever given a one-man show at the Smith College Museum of Art, among other important exhibitions. The time was notable particularly for a developing friendship with two elderly sisters, Bette and Agnes Mongan, who were influential curators and much-respected powerhouses in art circles. One of Hannock's most famous paintings, *The Oxbow, After Church, After Cole, Flooded*—his reinterpretation of Thomas Cole's famous 1836 painting of the oxbow-shaped excrescence of the Connecticut River near Northampton—carries the subtitle *Flooded River for the Matriarchs: E. & A. Mongan.* It is Hannock's homage to two women who instructed him to learn his art history and tradition, and who, he says today, "led me through the minefields for twenty years." Their advice to him in the early 1980s was simple: "Go to New York."

The center of the global art world, yes. Still, New York City might seem an odd choice for a painter whose work brings to life the most expansive of landscapes, and rejoices in all the natural forces so absent from the city. Indeed, the contrast between what's going on outside in Soho and what's going on inside Hannock's tenth-floor studio at the corner of Broadway and Houston Street is sharp. Outside is the whole hurly-burly of lower Manhattan: traffic, pedestrians, streetside vendors, grappling and pulsing through a spiky urban vista. Inside is yet another nocturne-in-progress, yet another winterscape, yet another sensual, silent scene devoid of people. Outside, on a giant billboard, are the ample, thrusting buttocks of black singer Foxy Brown, tightly packed into a pair of Calvin Klein jeans, prepared to "give it up." Inside is a personal Arcadia: here a tiny miniature of forest, an enticement of mauves and corals; there a bed-sized flooded-river scene, aloof and cryptic in silver, forest green, and blue.

The studio—twenty-five feet by forty feet—is casually ordered, friendly, efficient; Hannock occasionally sleeps here, and his golf clubs, for forays away, peek from behind a rack of his clothing. "Over here makin' a mess," he says cheerfully, leaving a phone message for a friend; "Cool and groovy vibes upon you and your household," he tells another; "It's your favorite artist, just checkin' in," he informs a third. He screens his calls, of course, occasionally grabbing the phone to lapse into a pronounced Scottish accent with the closest cronies. "Aye," he roars to one ferociously, "ye have found me in Splashville. It's true!"

The studio is his home, his temple, his retreat. It is his sanctuary of productivity, of vision. Outwardly he is boyish and playful; but inwardly, he is remarkably focused and tenaciously single-minded, a hockey player protecting the goal of making his life's work with paint. "I go to great pains to surround myself with relative simplicity," he says, a remark that can be read as both observation and caution.

The art in this book must speak for itself. But understanding the process by which it's created and what Hannock is specifically trying to achieve will help readers who may have little direct access to the originals. The lion's share of the paintings reproduced here represent the artist's mature phase, best captured by the description that accompanies their display: "polished oil on canvas." Or, more precisely, "many layers of polished paint and resin on canvas."

Hannock begins by knifing a modeling paste onto canvas. "If I was interested in an ultimately smooth surface," he explains, "I'd use Masonite." But canvas, with its slightly uneven texture, gives him the opportunity to exploit "accidents," the unexpected ways that paste, paint, and resin can seep into and fill the spaces in the fabric, and thus affect the colors and even the direction of a painting. He then stains the modeling paste by putting pigments into it to trace the design of his subject, which might be an aqueduct, a flooded river, or an apparent abstraction that is, in fact, squid boats sending up evening flares over the China Sea, an inspiration from a long trip through Asia. "The act of polishing the paint happens through different layers," he says. "The paint is built up after the modeling paste is set, and then transparent resins are applied and polished after they are set. They're built up again and then polished so that there's a substantial thickness of transparent surface between the layers of paint."

More paint, more resin, more polishing, the polishing doing its own creative part. "The act of building up paint and polishing down into it to create a smooth surface that totally possesses the desired light is an interesting act that is fraught with accidents. It's precisely these accidents that fascinate me. Painting these trees, hills, riverbanks, whatever, in gestures that are then polished, chunks of the paint fly off or are scraped away. It's an event so random that you can't possibly calculate or manipulate it."

What he can manipulate is what's left. Technically, the direct effect is almost sculptural: "I try to calculate the layering of paint in a way that almost creates a relief suspended in paint," he says. The result is like the texture of the effigy slightly raised above the surface of a coin. More paint, more resin, more polishing, a process repeated as many as a dozen times, "until the piece just speaks to you, that whatever further effort might go into it can't improve the painting."

The wet-dry sandpaper Hannock employs ranges in grit from 220 to 400, a gradation that he has learned by process of trial-and-error. Early on, some smaller canvases actually exploded when he tried sandpaper without the lubrication of water or a diluted resin. "There was nothing left," he laughs. Sanding by hand doesn't work either, he notes; "it winds up being done too carefully." He points to James McNeill Whistler, himself a painter of nocturnes, who would have his assistants scrape down his emerging paintings at a key phase of their gestation. The virtue of the assistants, Hannock explains, was that they were merciless, unaffected by any emotional bond with the work. So is the sander. "Every so often, I'll create a lyrical moment," Hannock says, "and the temptation is just to lightly sand and be careful in that area. But that's against the rules. What happens to the overall canvas aesthetically when the piece is polished as a whole yields a much more successful work of art than if I go over these little spotted areas carefully. Ultimately, the work of art is less strong if you're fussy with it."

He holds his outstretched fingers close to the dark foreground water of a beautiful finished nocturne hung on the ample wall space. At a fraction of an inch away, the fingernails are clearly reflected, the reflection dissolving as he pulls them just farther back. "That's perfect," he judges. "The surface is crisp enough that you can see through the paint, but it's not so hyper-glossy that it's going to be reflecting the viewer's own image, particularly with the darker sections."

Hannock is probably the last man in Soho with a squeegee, the infamous windshield wipers having long since been banished by Mayor Rudolph Giuliani. Now he's using it to wipe down the surface of the nocturne and let it set yet again. He's satisfied at its evolution; the details haven't snagged him either, as they sometimes can. He points to a gorgeous flooded-river scene on the other side of the room in which the trees literally hover in the water. A tiny fissure of cloud edges the neutral sky above. "That took a day to get right," he says of the creamy white wrinkle of paint, not unaffectionately.

Of all of God's fiats, the one Stephen Hannock would most easily agree with is: *fiat lux*—"let there be light." "I'm obsessed with light," he says. "I'm obsessed with everything light does. With how powerful it is and yet how fragile, how intense and yet how fleeting. One minute it's overwhelming, unbelievable, and the next minute, gone. The work is about what the paint can do to create the illusion of luminosity."

His remark is telling, a credo; that he utters it standing next to *Evening Launch for George* is telling, too. It was John Walsh, director of the J. Paul Getty Museum of Art, who introduced Hannock to the existence of a history of incendiary nocturnes when the painter was first moving in that direction. Prior to Whistler, seventeenth- and eighteenth-century artists created nocturnes principally to dazzle European courts with the fleeting impression of fireworks. "It was invigorating," Hannock says, "for me to find myself part of a tradition instead of sluggishly trying to pioneer something out of the blue."

He is part of a tradition, very clearly, but it isn't European: It's that of the nineteenth-century American landscapists usually grouped together as the Hudson River School and, within that larger school, that of the luminists. It would be very easy to fool even a knowledgeable public by hanging Hannocks in a show that included Cole, Church, Albert Bierstadt, John Frederick Kensett, and others. His lush landscapes, if slightly more brooding, would easily join theirs. Thomas Cole's observation from his "Essay on American Scenery" could practically be Hannock's own: "Another component of scenery without which every landscape is defective—water"; it's the rare Hannock canvas that doesn't feature water, doesn't glory in it. From any point of inquiry—geography, mood, technical assurance, composition, the exaltation of nature, the sheer scale which Gaston Bachelard once described as "intimate immensity"—Hannock would snuggle easily among painters who worked a full century-and-a-half or more earlier.

Narrow the perspective to what art historians call luminism, the movement that flourished in the United States between approximately 1850 and 1875, and the brotherhood still holds. In her penetrating essay "On Defining Luminism" Barbara Novak writes, "In lay parlance any painting in which light is the most expressive feature may be called *luminist*." That describes Hannock exactly. "The expressive impact," she writes, "is dependent on the glassy surface, which transforms paint into a substance that shines and emanates." Hannock again, with his "polished oil on canvas." "A key correlative of luminism is silence," Novak writes, posing luminism as an opposite to Impressionism, in which the painter with his evident brush strokes literally paints himself into the picture and thus interposes his persona between viewer and subject. By contrast, the luminist painter excises the evidence of his brush strokes, and thus of himself. Luminist, thy name is Hannock.

Up to a point. "These guys had a lot of baggage about being true to nature," he says. "In this arena, we don't give a damn; it's all about the paint." Look closely at nineteenth-century luminist canvases, and a viewer will usually see precise geography, not just rendered but noted: Kaaterskill Falls, Lake George, Mount Washington, and the great mother lode—the Hudson River—and its transcendental radiant light. But look closely at almost any Hannock landscape and ask yourself where you are. Outwardly, the geography seems familiar, his "trees, hills, riverbanks, whatever." You could be . . . where? In fact you're in the painter's imagination, in his narrative reordering of what he has physically witnessed.

"For me," says Hannock firmly, "landscape is not about topography. It's least about topography. With me it's about using primordial objects to create a very fundamental and simple composition that light can be hung on. It's an excuse to make a lightscape. Everything from my most abstract nocturnes, squid-boat paintings, and incendiary nocturnes to the fastidious and almost historical paintings—the Oxbow and the Great Falls at Yellowstone, which are quite literal landscapes—what they have in common is that they're lightscapes. The landforms themselves are just devices that break the conceptual surface of the painting and allow us to go through and essentially be drawn in by the light."

Traditionalist, modern man. A man not just of a new century but of a new millennium. Hannock will pay conscious homage to nineteenth-century painters in nocturnes such as *Evening Launch for George*; he'll also reinterpret nineteenth-century paintings such as Cole's to show off the technical bravura that has established him as one of America's leading landscapists. He took on the Oxbow, he says, "because I thought I could paint a better painting." Of his own nocturnes versus the eighteenth-century versions: "Because of the polishing the light is more sophisticated." Yes, his shelves are crowded with volumes of the work of his aesthetic forebears—Albert Pinkham Ryder, Louis Rémy Mignot, Thomas Moran, and especially the towering British genius J. M. W. Turner, among others. But as he toils away merrily with his electric sander, while a screensaver mutates on the computer behind him, and the sound system pours Sarah Vaughan, Branford Marsalis, and Erroll Garner into the room, it's clear that Stephen Hannock has no desire to turn back the clock.

The life Hannock leads today is really exactly as he would choose it. He's not rich, but finally secure. He works with the kind of pressure that artists appreciate, pleasing a public that cannot get enough of him. His troika of dealers in New York, Houston, and San Francisco see that no paintings languish; that there are three dealers and not one is by design, to ensure also that the pool of Hannock collectors widens. It's rumored that an outside dealer offered to buy two years of Hannock's work sight unseen for a lip-smacking sum; even though the painter will neither confirm or deny it, the concept is only superficially tempting. Hannock's career is still very much on an upward arc; the Metropolitan Museum of Art, for example, acquired its first painting, *Vortex At Dawn: Collapsed Light* in 1993, and wants another. To limit his production to one dealer's stable of clients would effectively truncate its reach. No thanks; not now.

With an engaging and amiable personality, and natural charisma, Hannock moves easily in the many worlds his collectors have introduced him to. His work is prized by leading restaurateur Danny Meyer, who has used large

Hannock canvases to define the ambience in two of his celebrated New York restaurants, the Gramercy Tavern and Eleven Madison Park. In any given season the painter may just be back from visiting rock star Sting and his wife, producer Trudie Styler, at their English country home; or anchorman Tom Brokaw and his wife, Meredith, on their sprawling Montana ranch; or professional football coach Bill Belichick at a team training session; the trips are an escape from the confinements of New York City as well as opportunities to sketch from nature. He plays golf with his father, Marshall, and basks in the gaze of his sister, Sally, and his mother, Liz, who still has his first art project—not for sale—and has always seen her son's potential clearly. He's not so busy or obsessed that he can't leave the studio in mid-afternoon to catch a movie with his lady, Bridget Watkins. He understands what he does now very well, both his technique and the reality of his oeuvre.

Hannock is happy, but he's always been happy; that's the buoyancy of his persona. It serves him well. The easy-going nature that once made him such a good teammate also contributed to his being chosen for the most interesting diversion of his career so far—contributing technical effects to the motion picture *What Dreams May Come.*

Rather than a scenic designer, Hannock explains, director Vincent Ward "specifically wanted an artist who was used to bringing his own ideas to life. For the first time in filmmaking he wanted to define Heaven and Hell in terms of fine art." The director's plan was ambitious, to enact a tragic but ultimately redemptive screenplay in which actress Annabella Sciorra's character, an art conservator and a painter, yearns to be reunited with the husband and children taken from her too soon. Heaven, where Robin Williams, her screen husband, arrives, is literally a living painting that fell to Hannock to envision.

The narrative centerpiece of the film is a large triptych. Hannock says, "It paid homage"—naturally—"to Caspar David Friedrich's *Two Men Observing the Moon* with the tree in the foreground, and the armature of a composition that I based loosely around Glacier National Park where the Heaven sequence was filmed" [plate 15]. What Hannock did was to paint stills from the film as they were being created. "These," he explains, "would be passed on to a group of wizards I affectionately referred to as 'the merry band of geeks,' who would translate my brush strokes into the computer-generated brush strokes." This yielded the sequence that feels as if the viewer has walked into the painting, its strokes smearing even as Robin Williams moves.

It's fair to say that Hannock's work was one of the most successful things about the film, which tended to scare viewers off with its emotional darkness and often cryptic plot development. Indisputably the brightest spot about *What Dreams May Come* was that it won the Academy Award for Special Effects in 1999, an honor shared by the technical crew, including Hannock.

"It's another way of being recognized, another extension of my work," he says reflectively, staring out the studio's large windows at the grimy cityscape of lower Manhattan. There are a number of those extensions now, as success and reputation beget success and reputation. He will soon produce and direct a music video that will further utilize the painted world of special effects from *What Dreams May Come*. He is designing his first opera set, for *Mary Shelley*, a collaboration with librettist Debora Atherton and composer Alan Jaffe, for an intended premiere in 2001. And, when appropriate, he undertakes striking photoassemblage works with Graham Nash and Mac Holbert that are at once playful and arresting.

There is a clear center, however, about which he is definite. It involves a brush, a sander, the crowded contents of his work trays, and a canvas. That it's a low-tech approach in a high-tech time, that it's an old-tech approach in a new-tech time, don't bother him any. "Ultimately," says Stephen Hannock, "the act of bringing ideas to life with paint on canvas is the most immediate. There is the least amount of interference. You get an idea and put it down, and nobody gets in your way. And that is a remarkably exhilarating feeling."

—Duncan Christy

Rhinebeck, New York

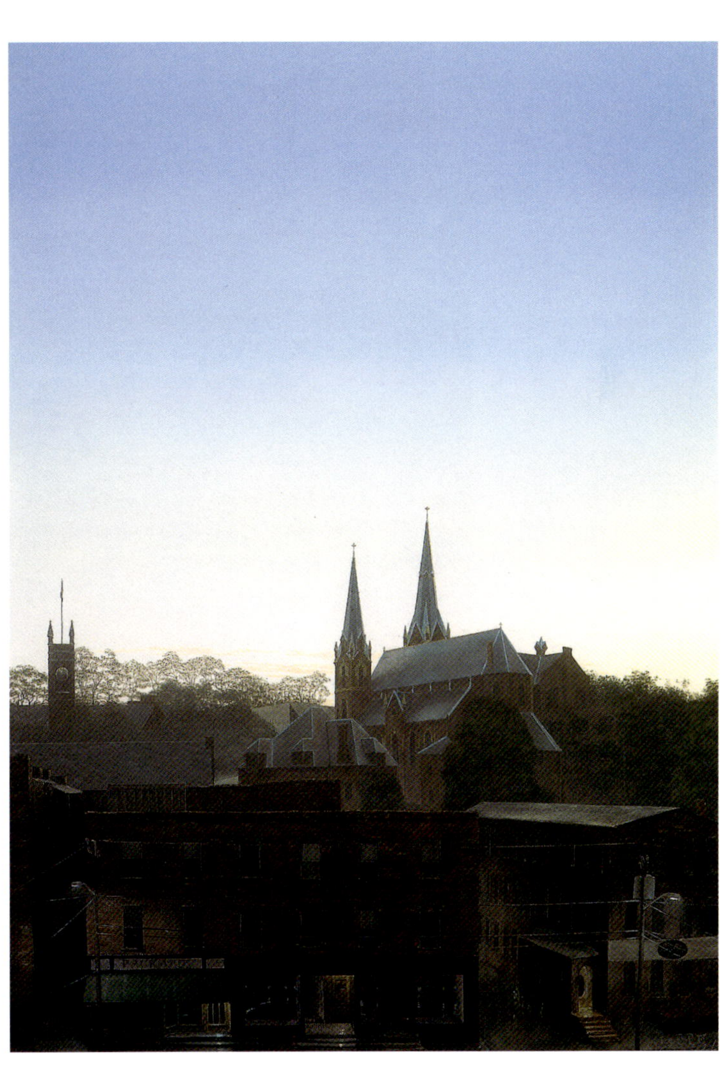

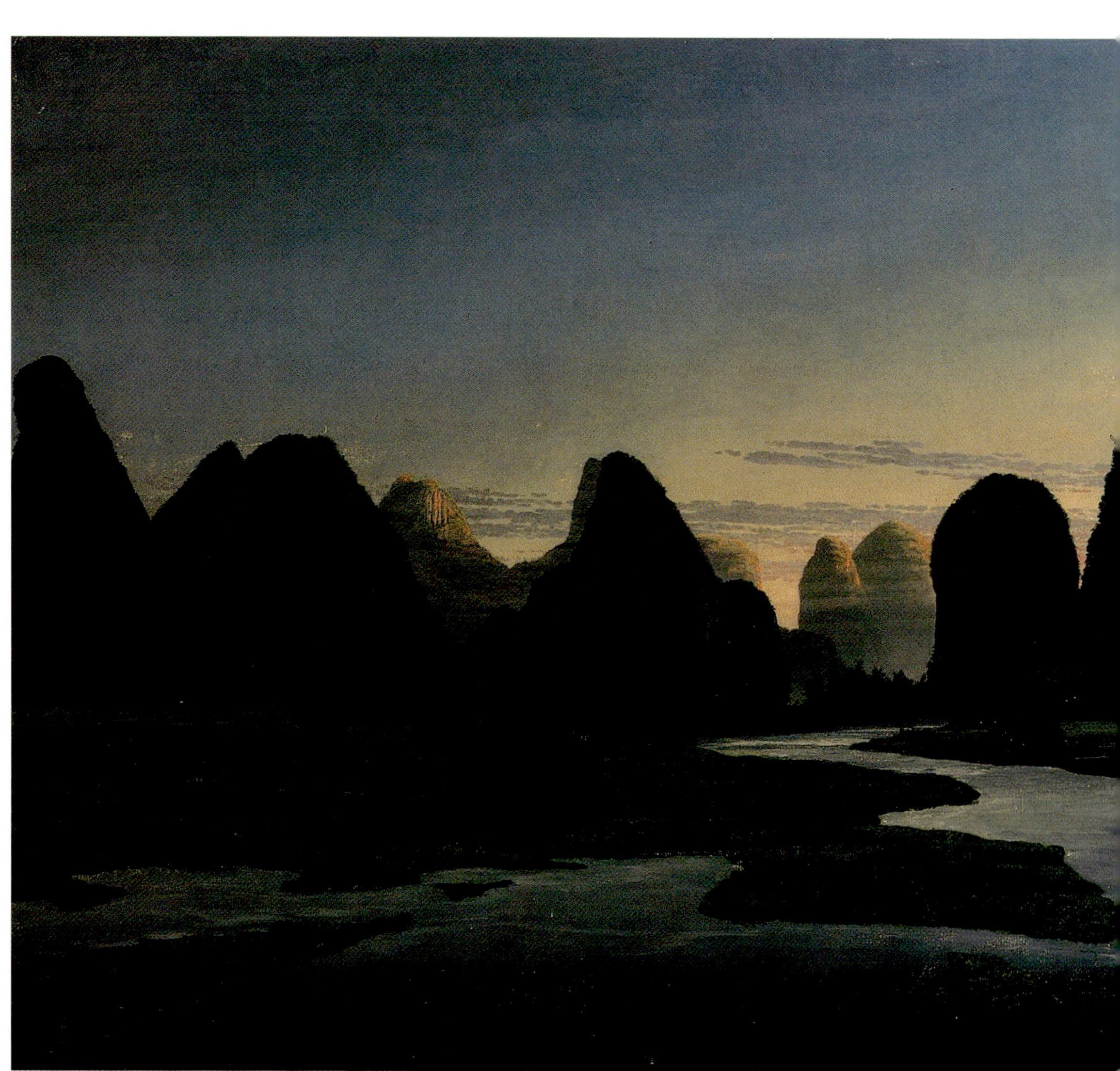

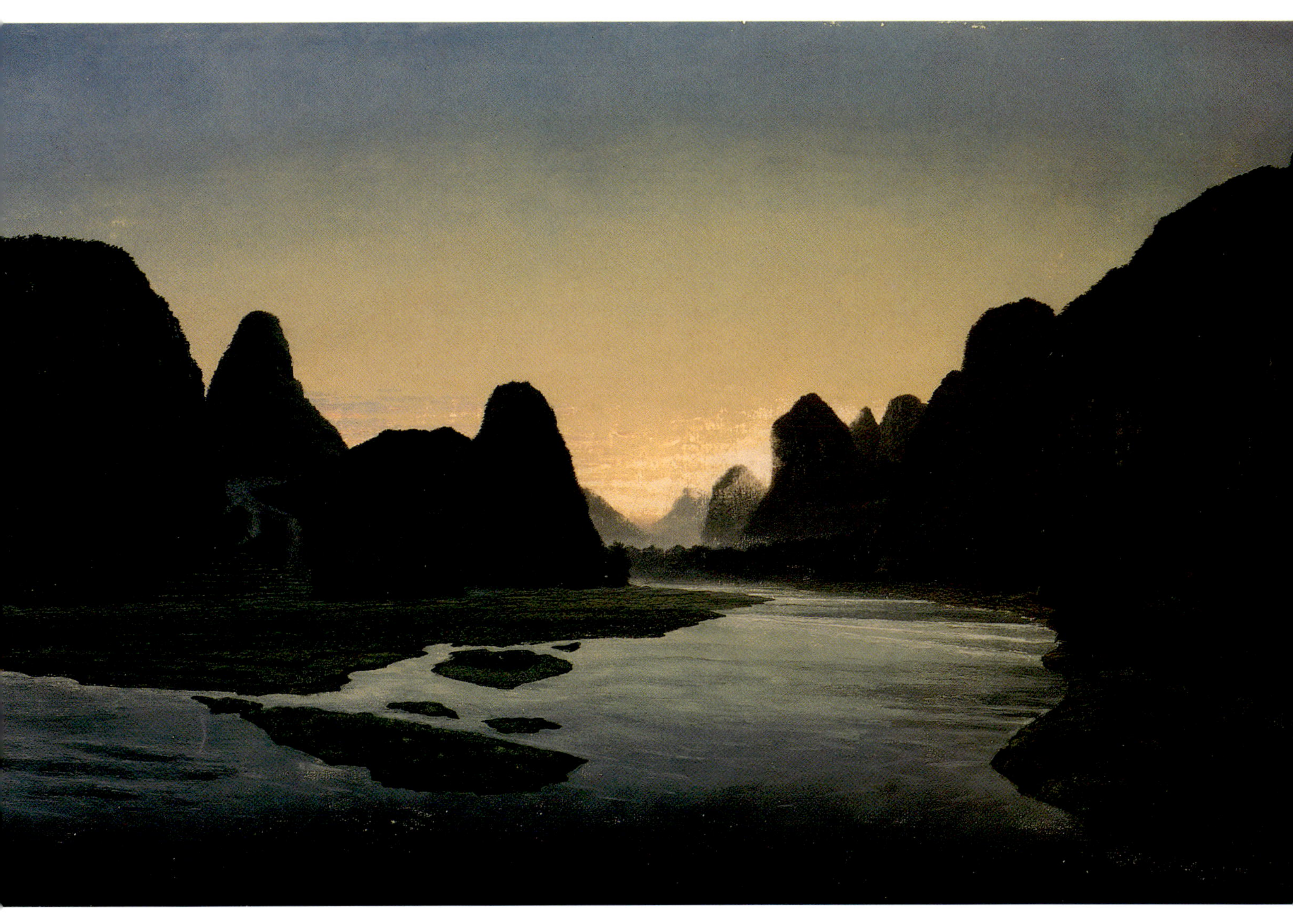

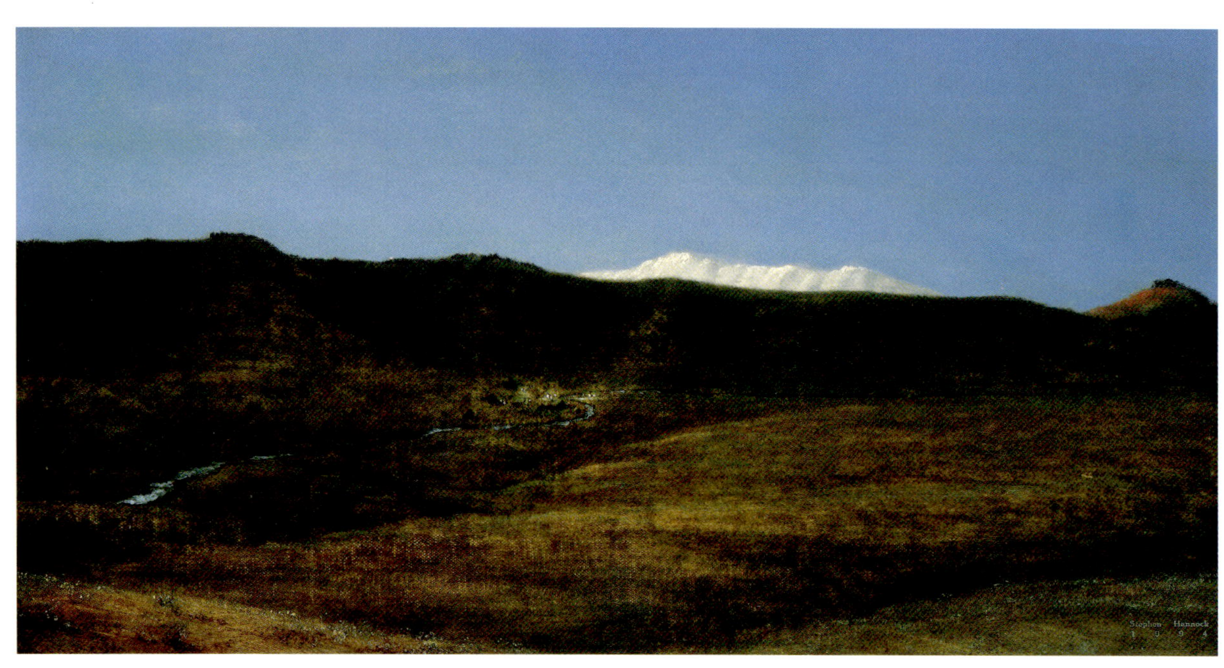

3 | 4

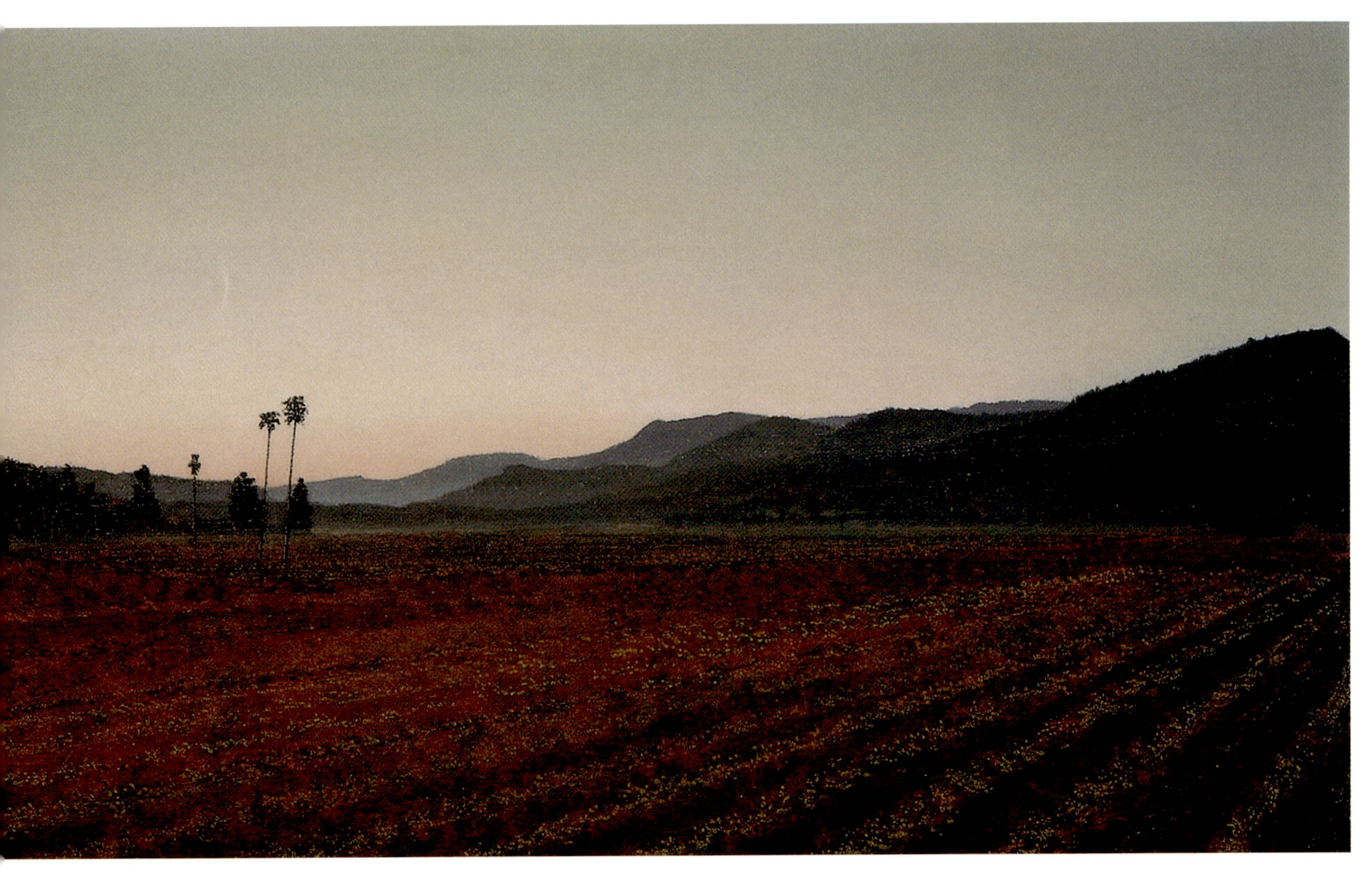

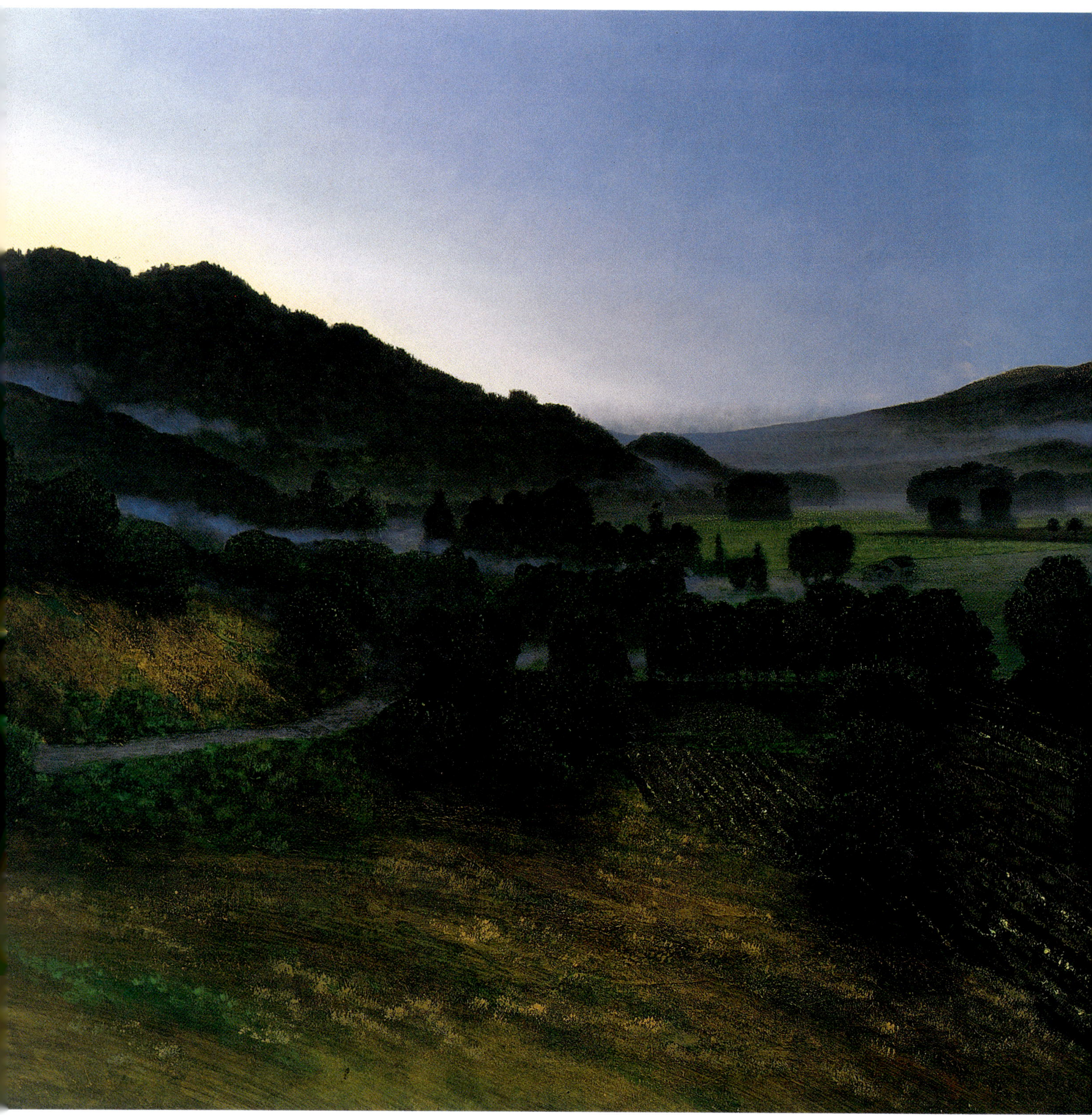

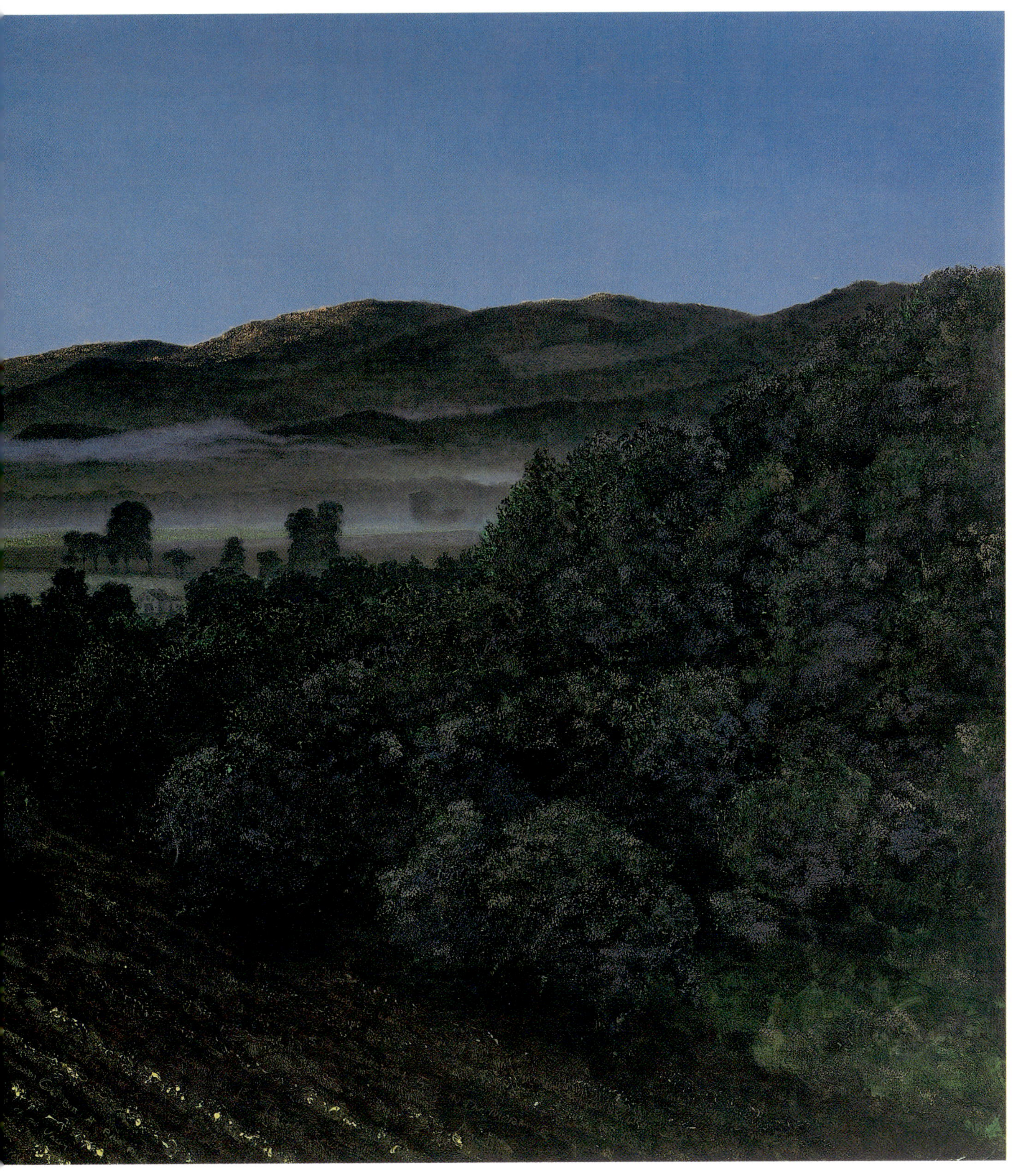

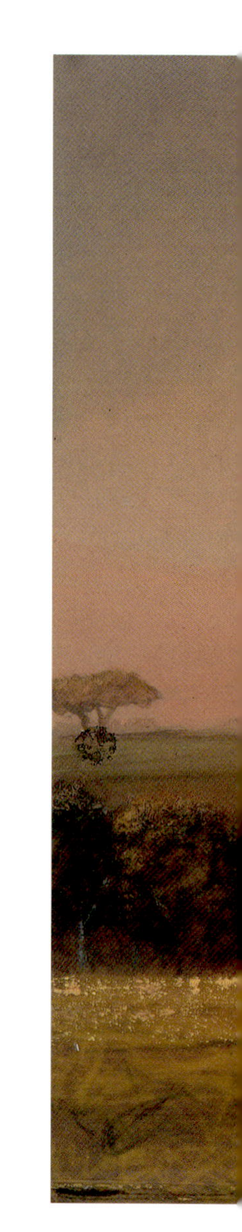

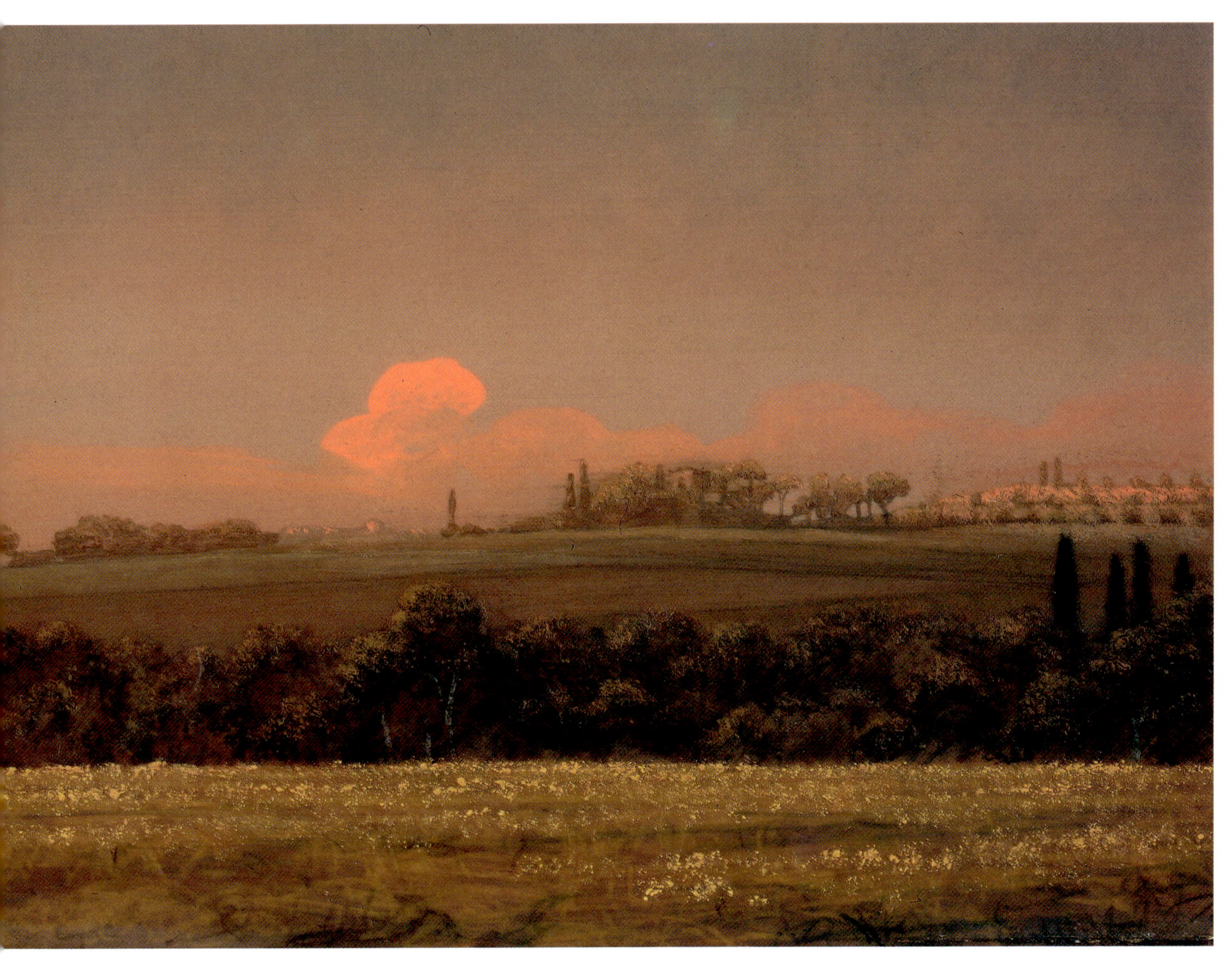

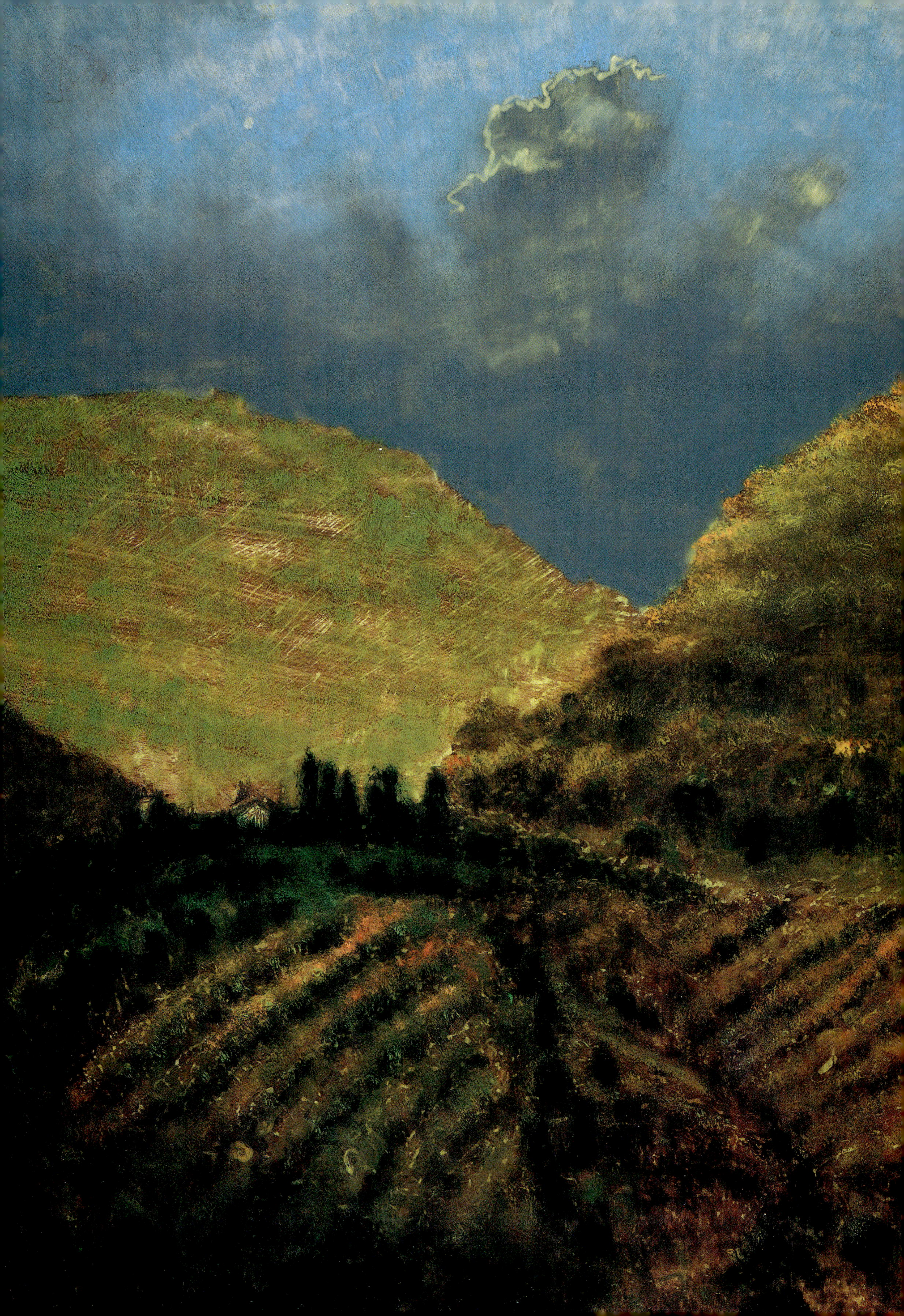

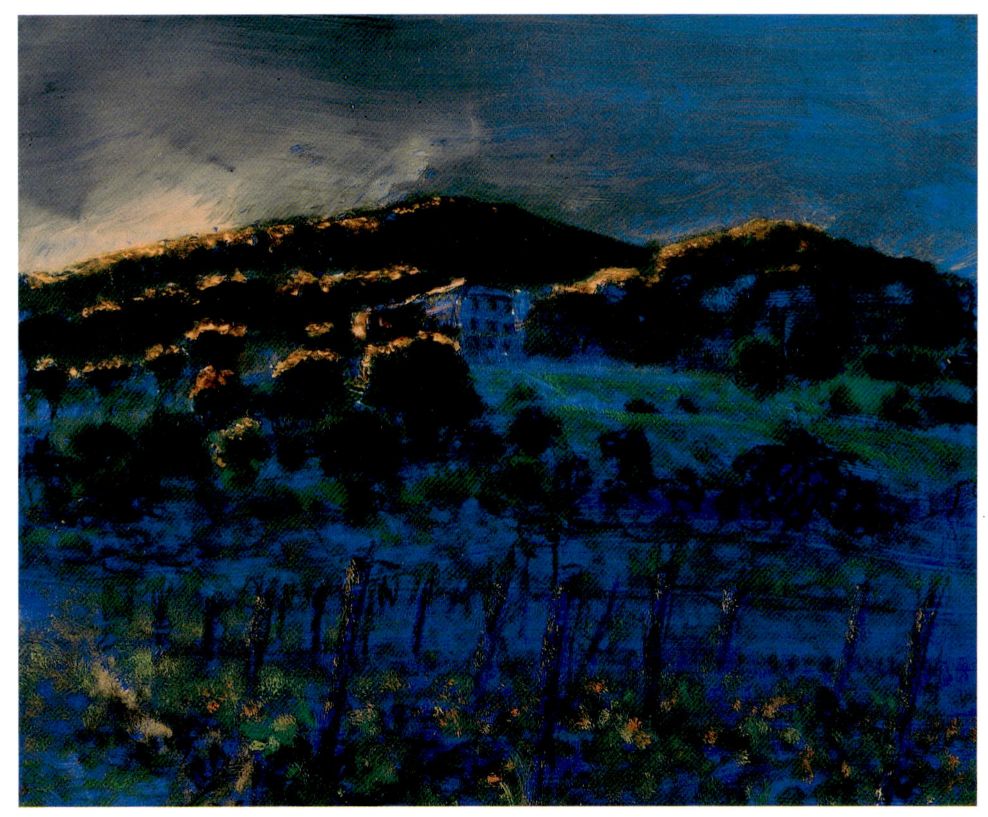

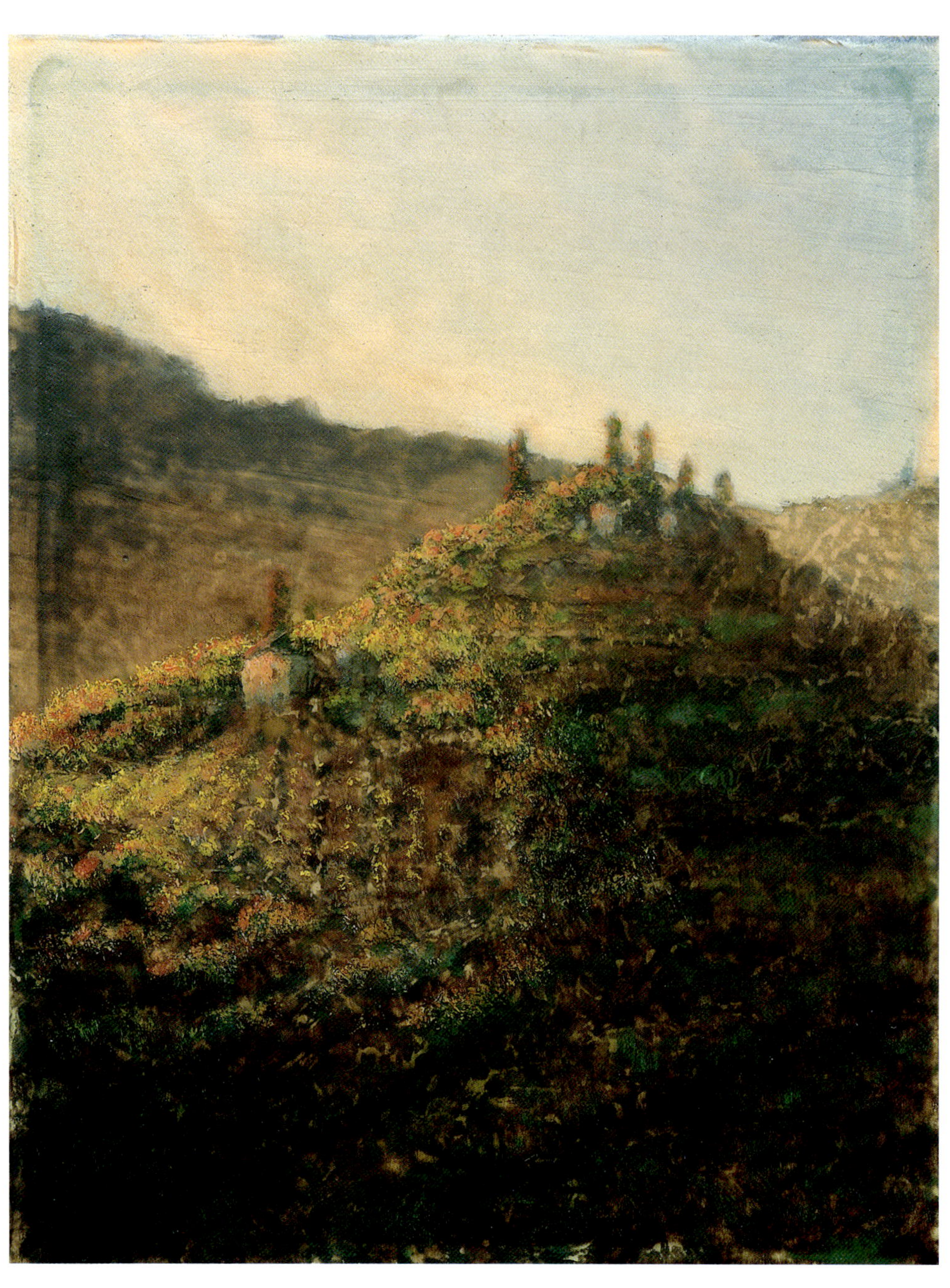

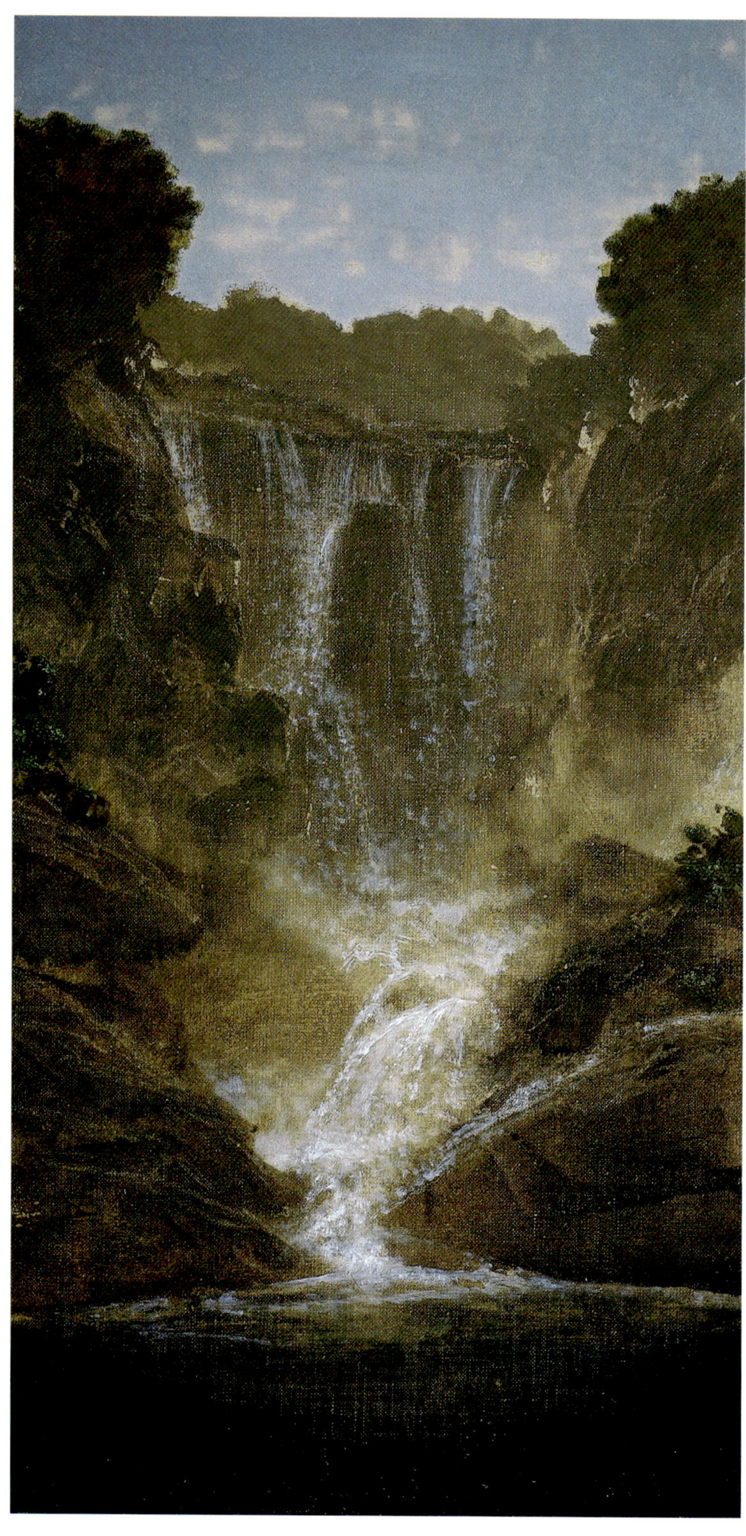

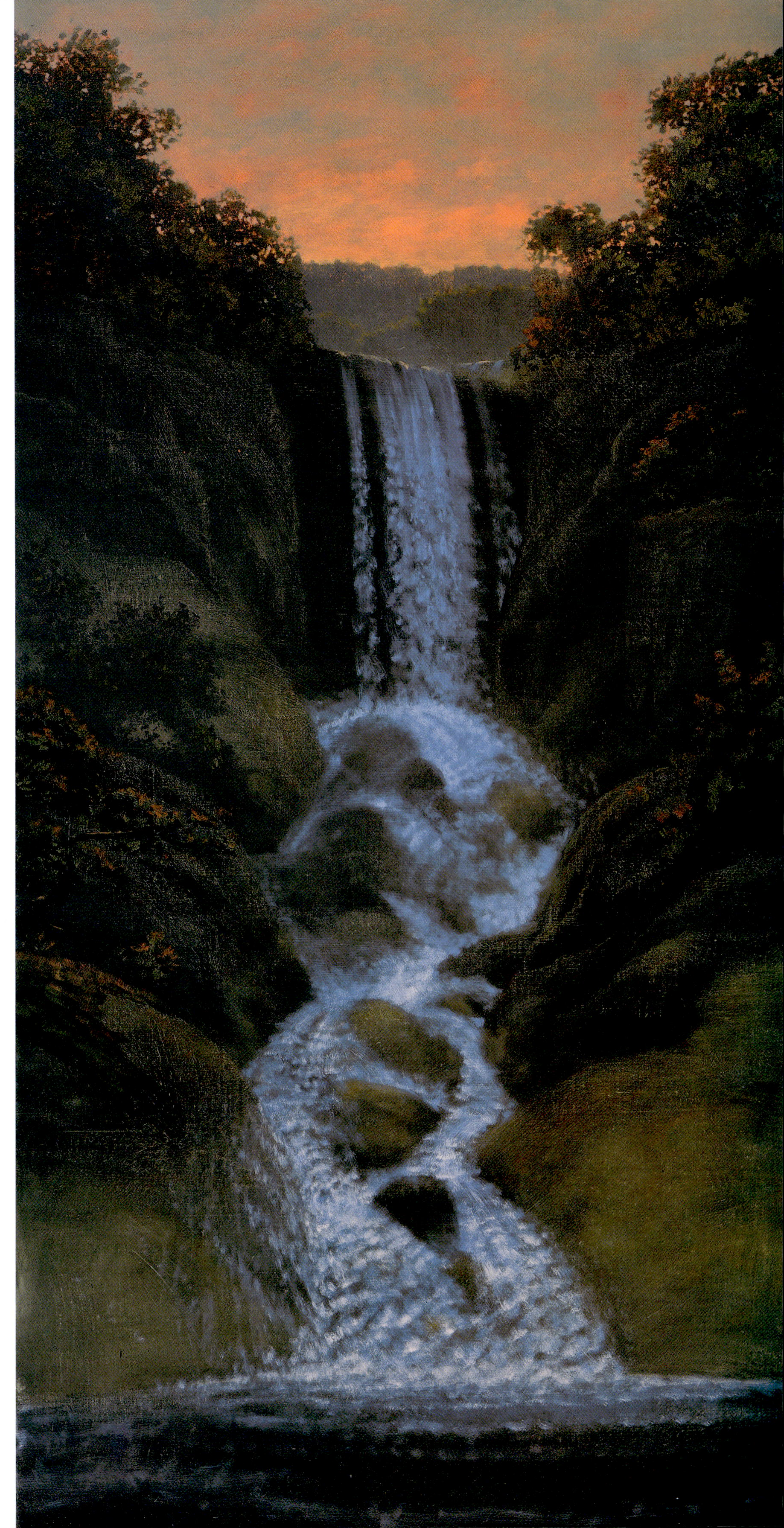

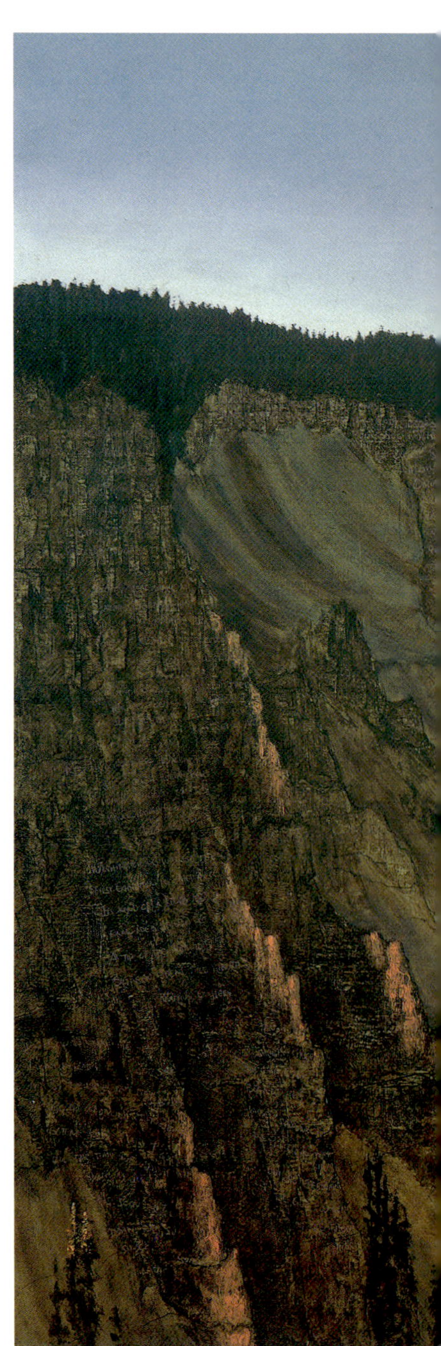

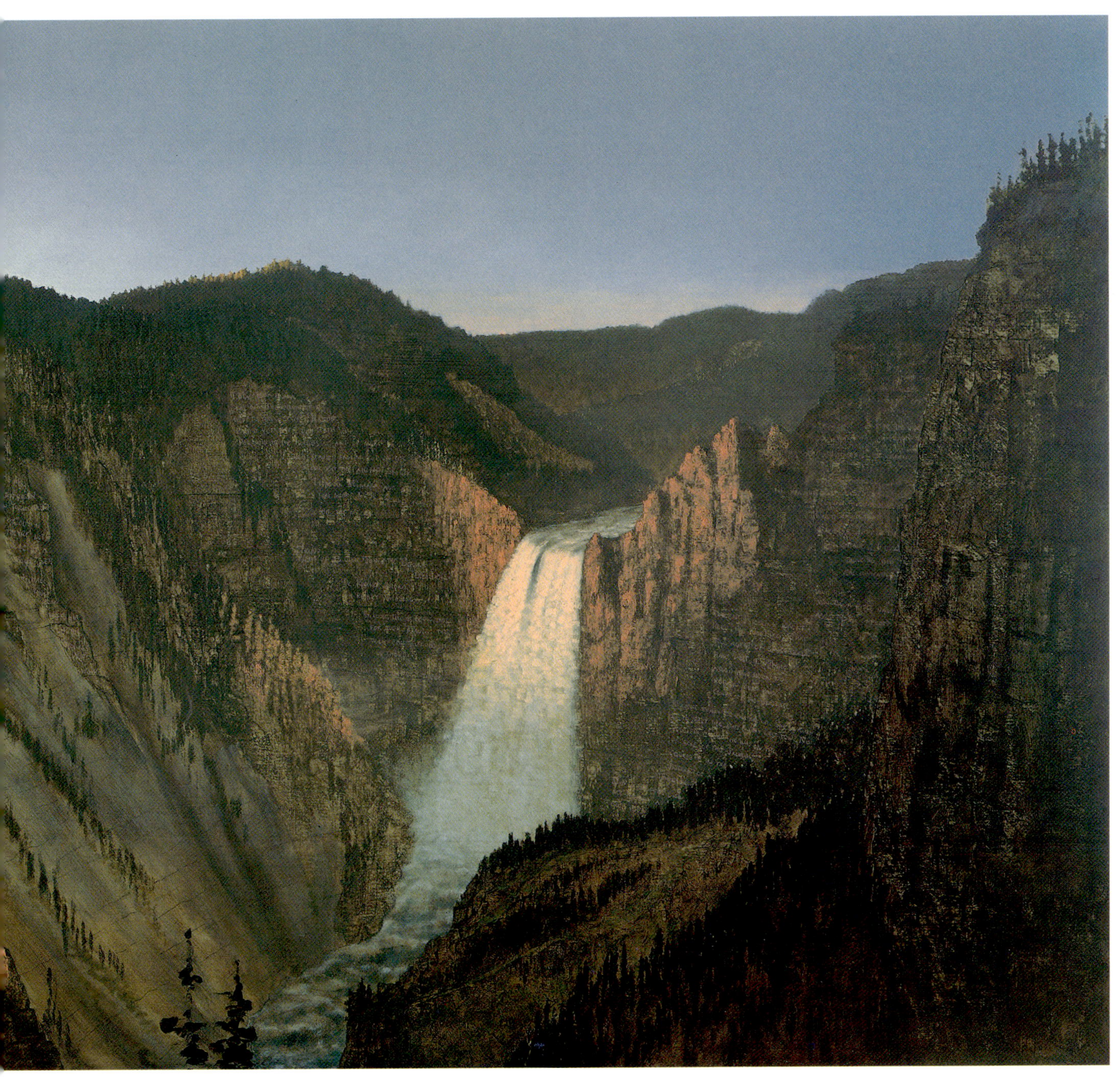

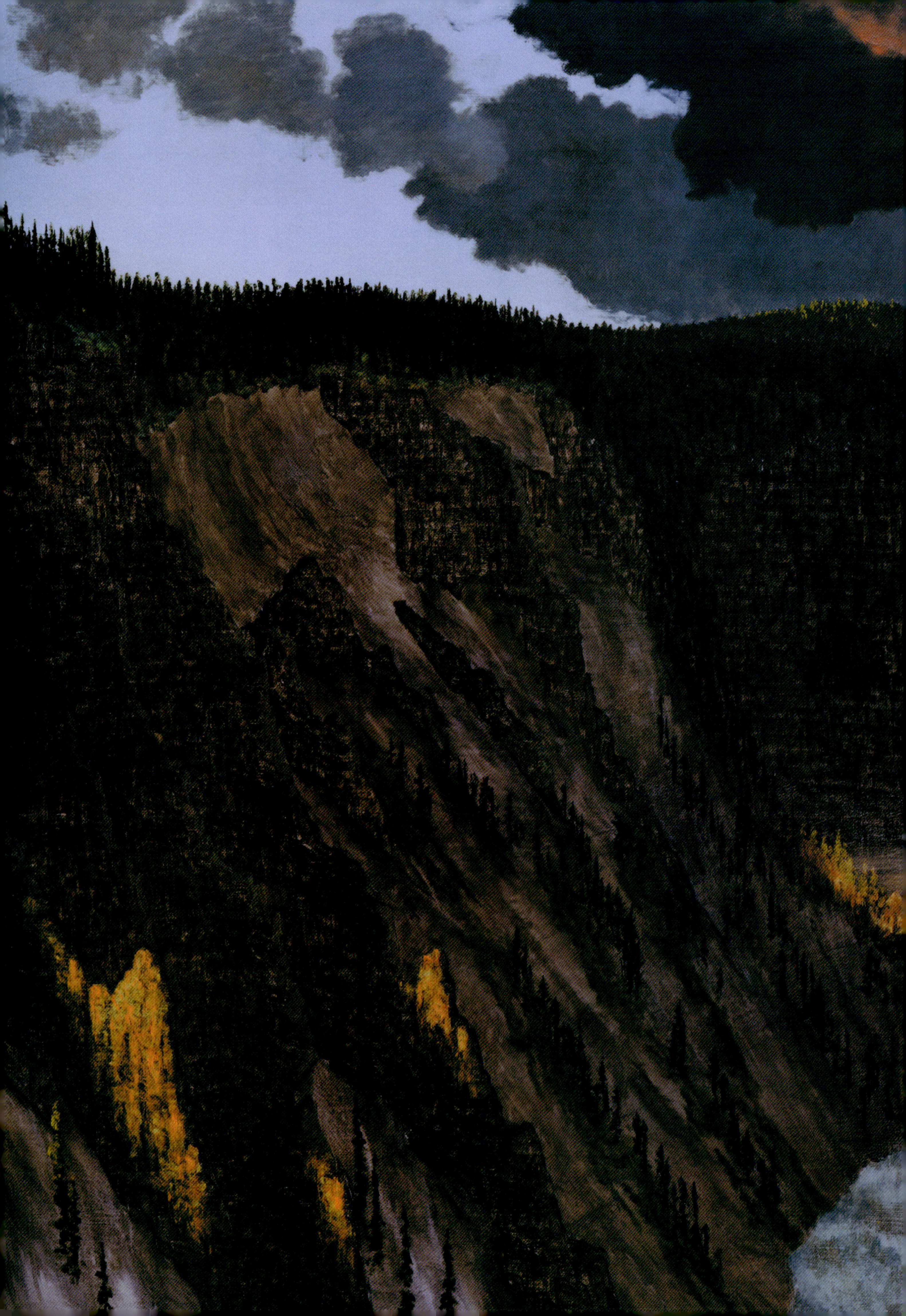

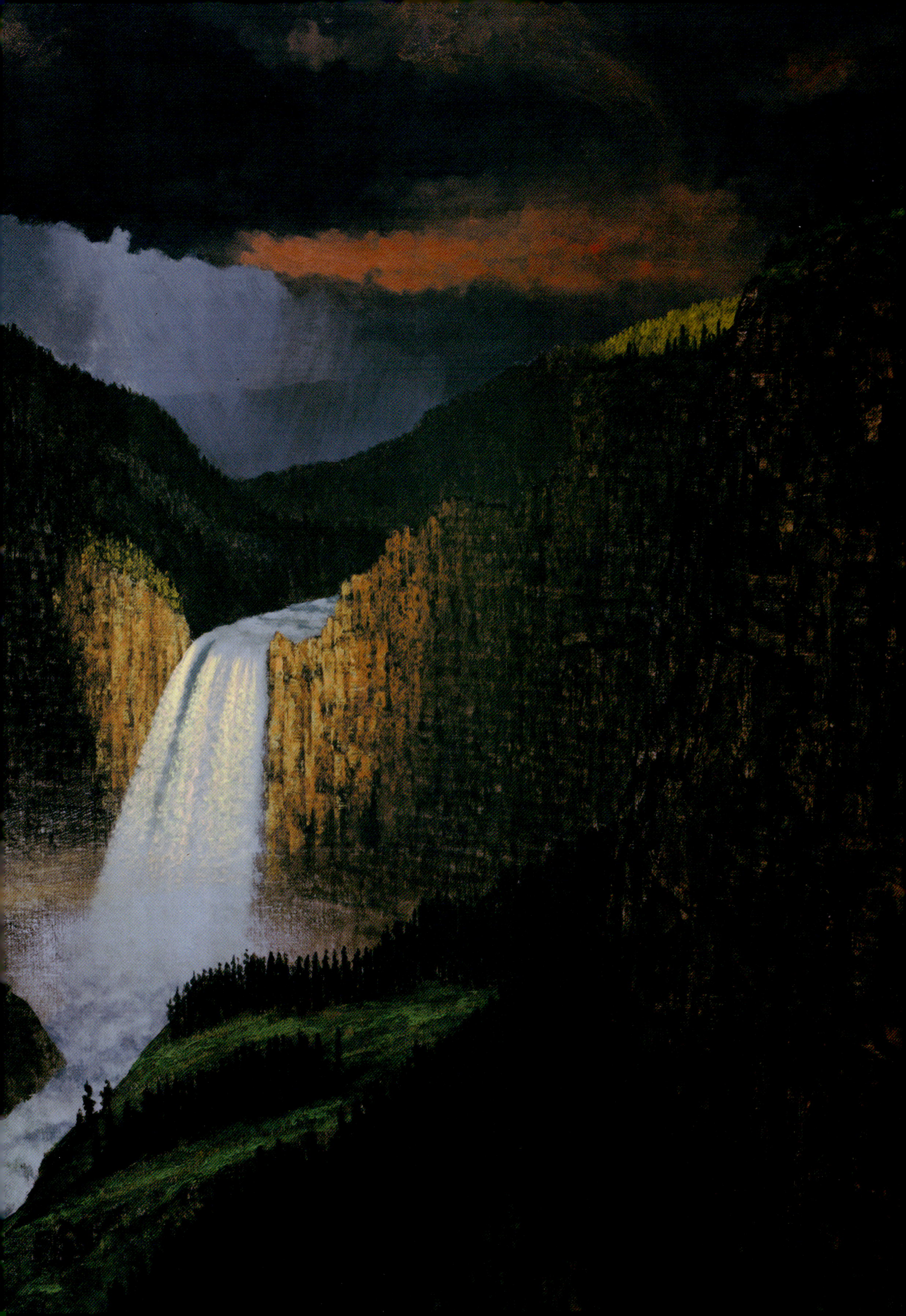

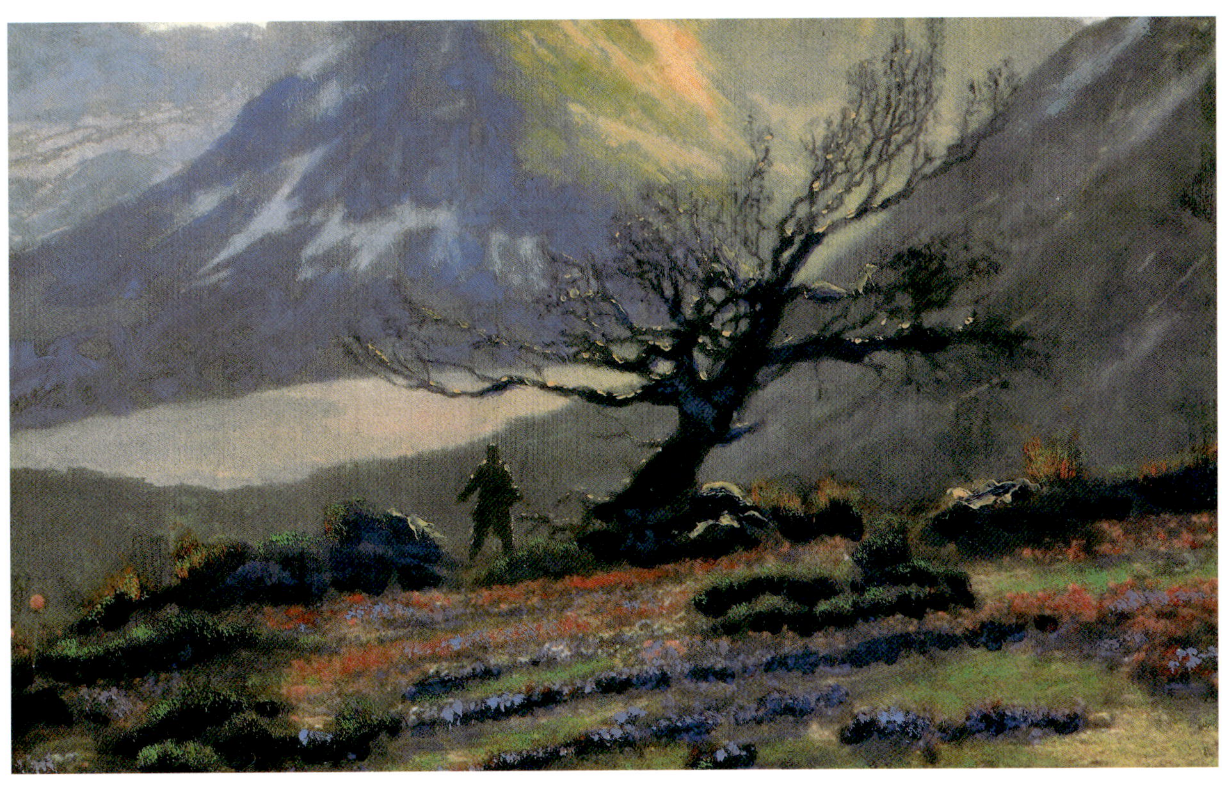

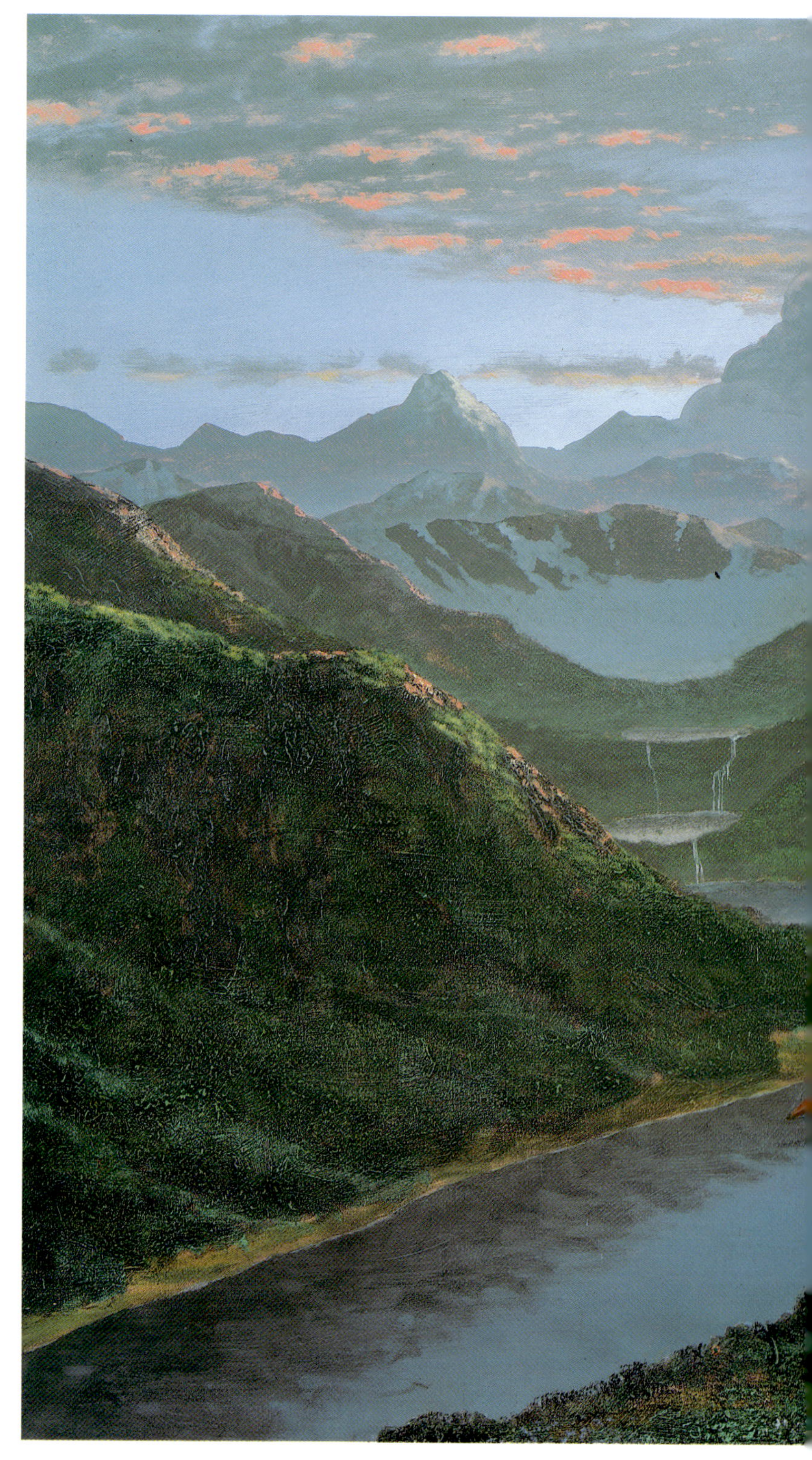

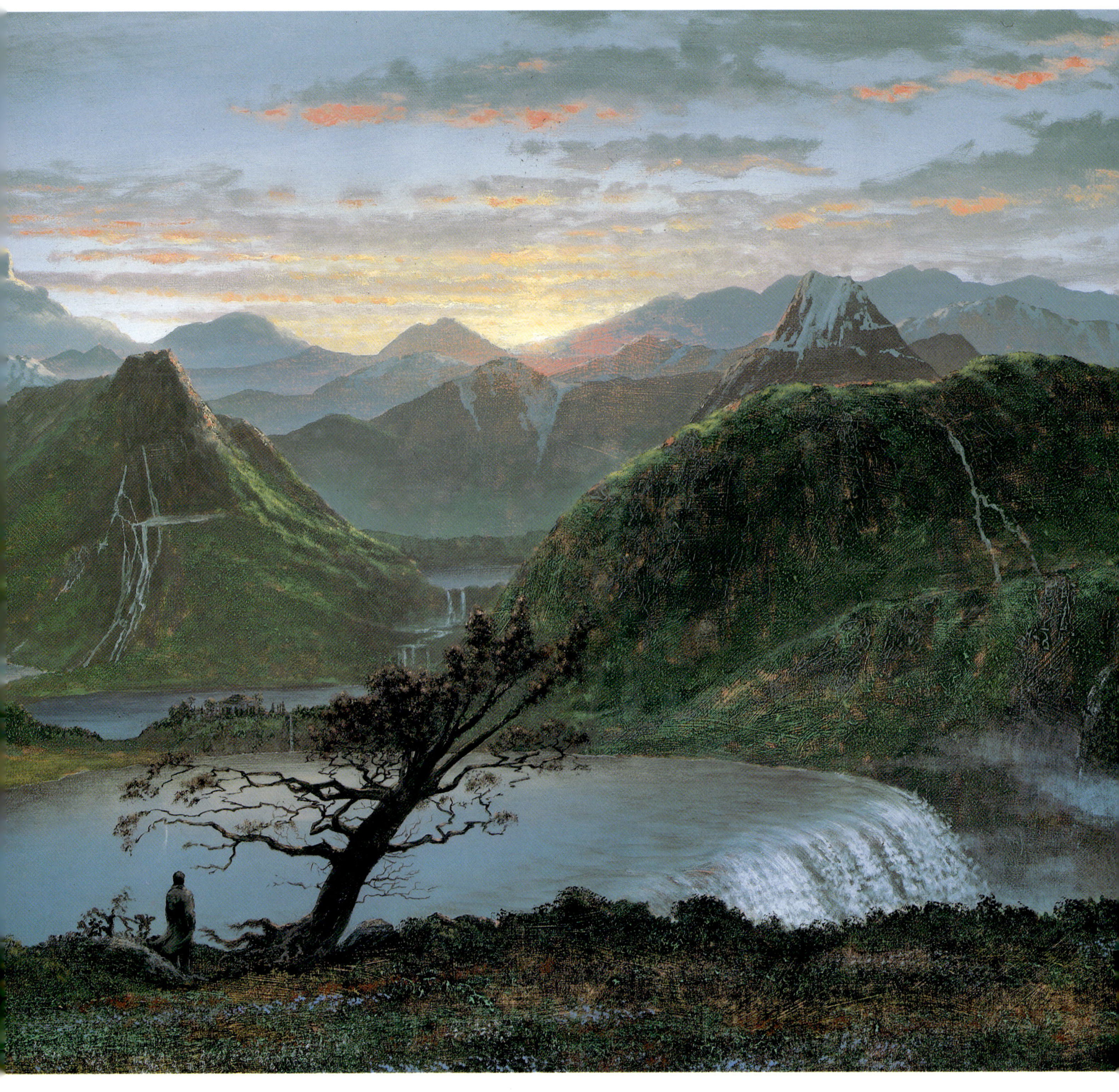

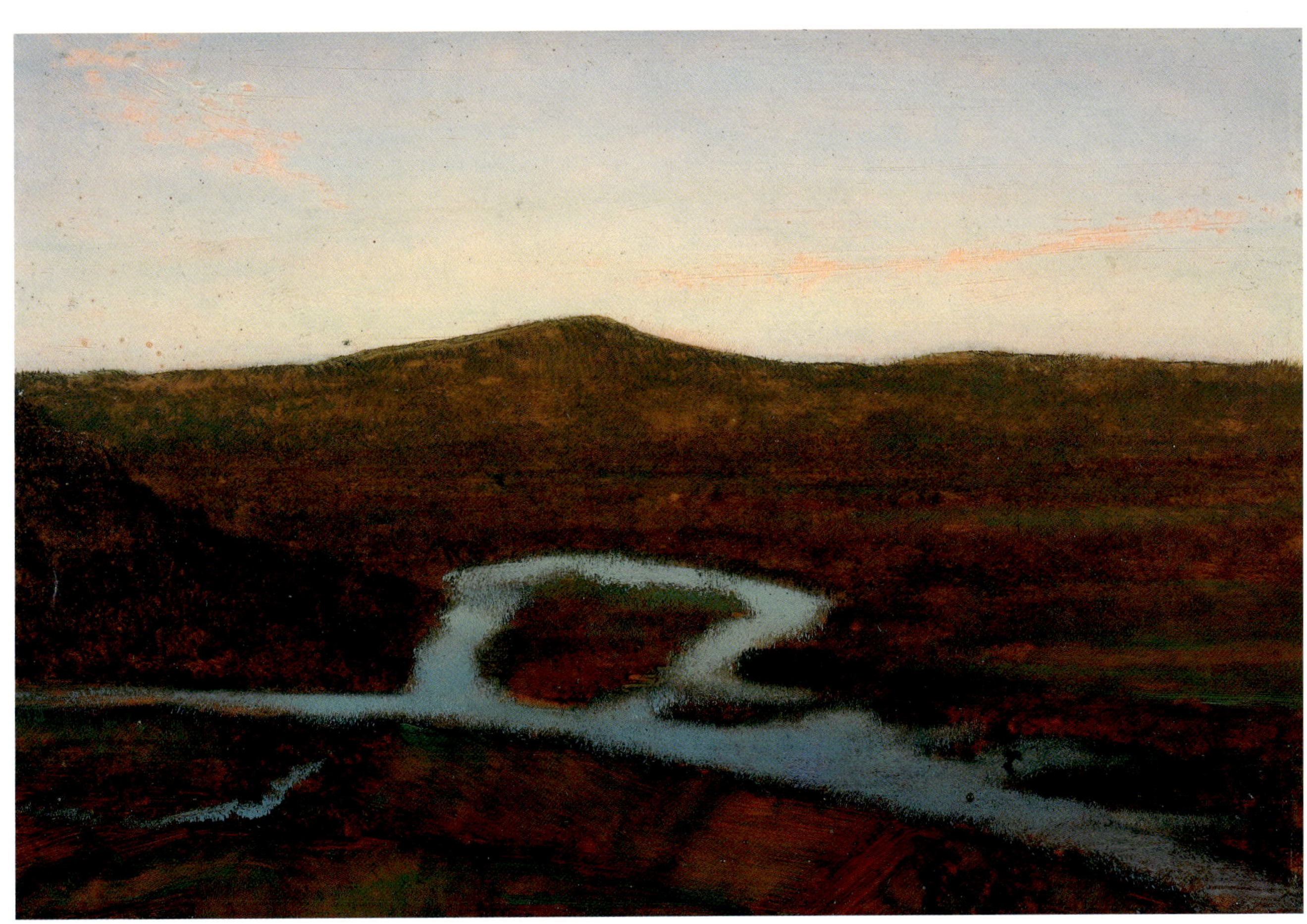

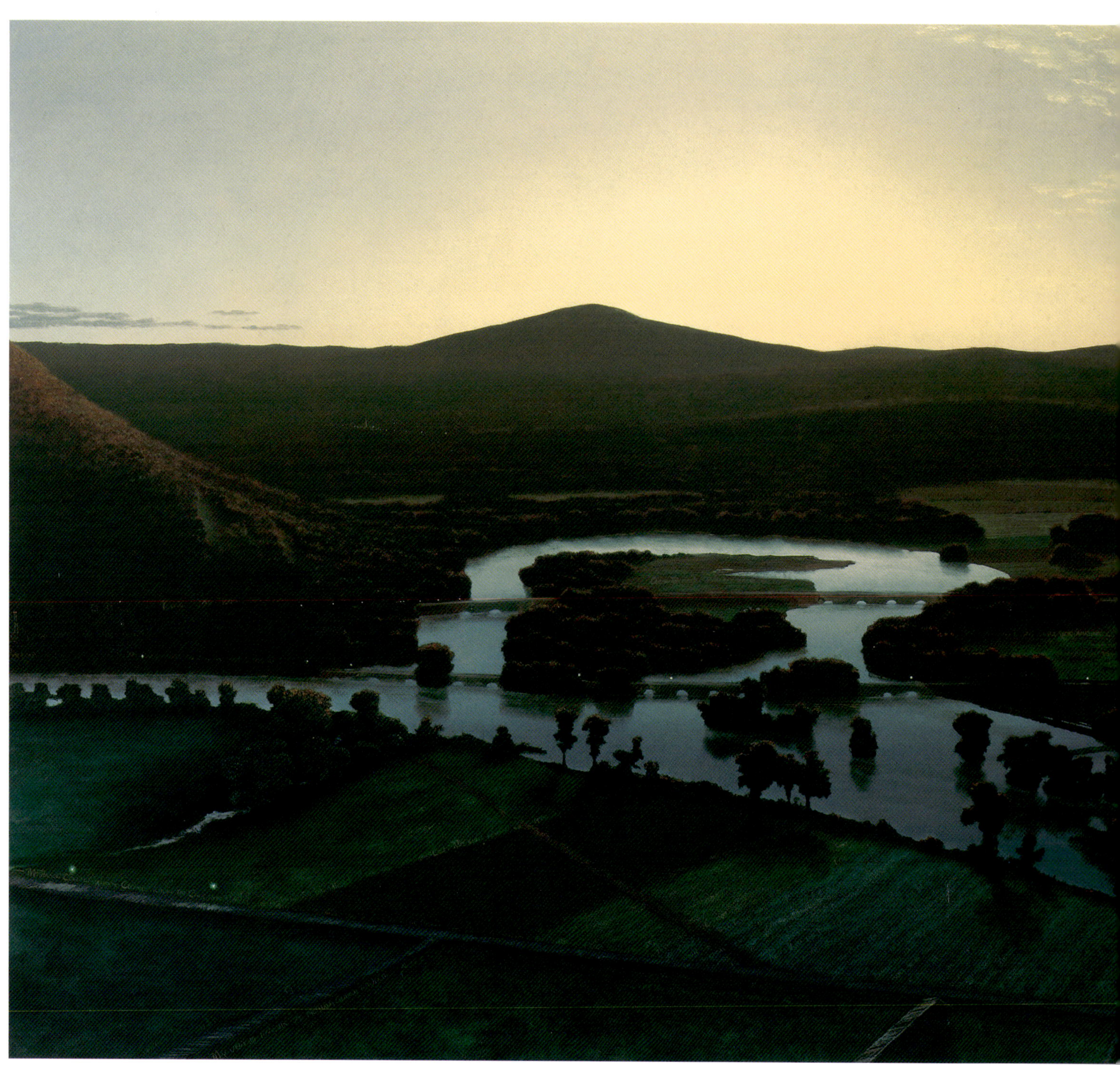

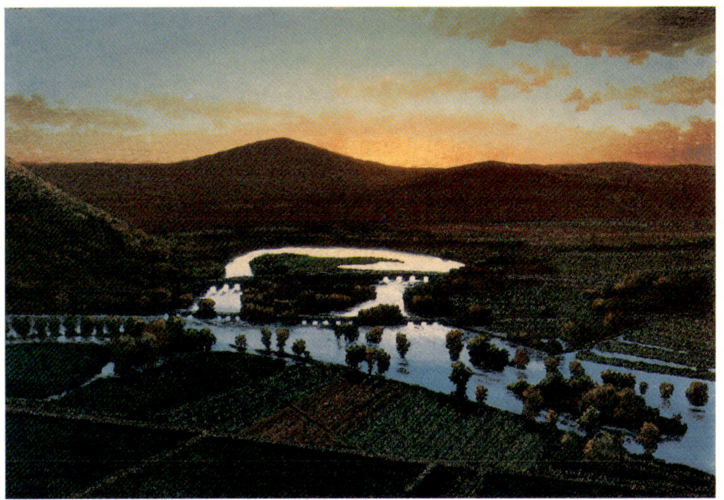

17 | 18 | 19

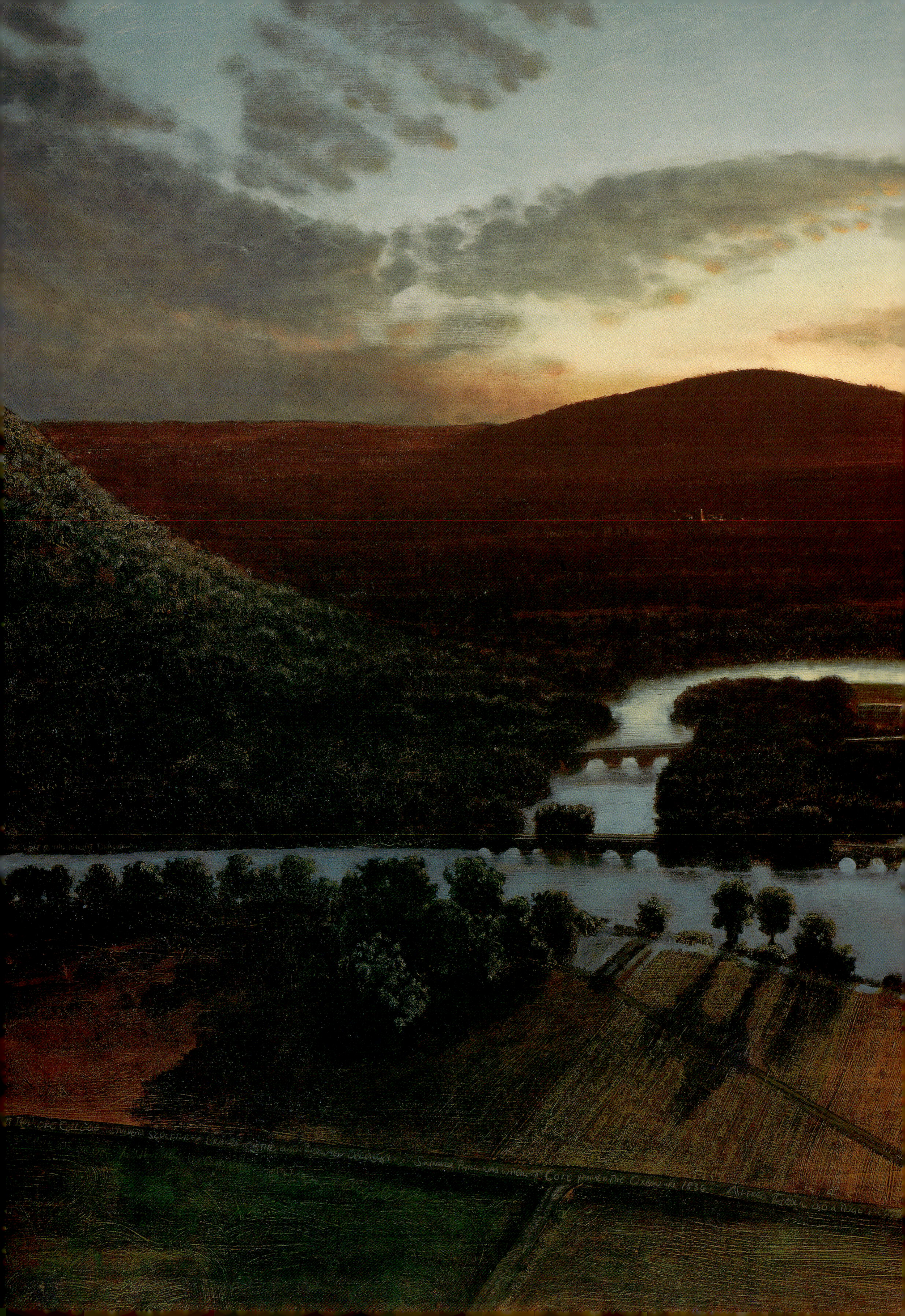
Cole painted the Oxbow in 1836

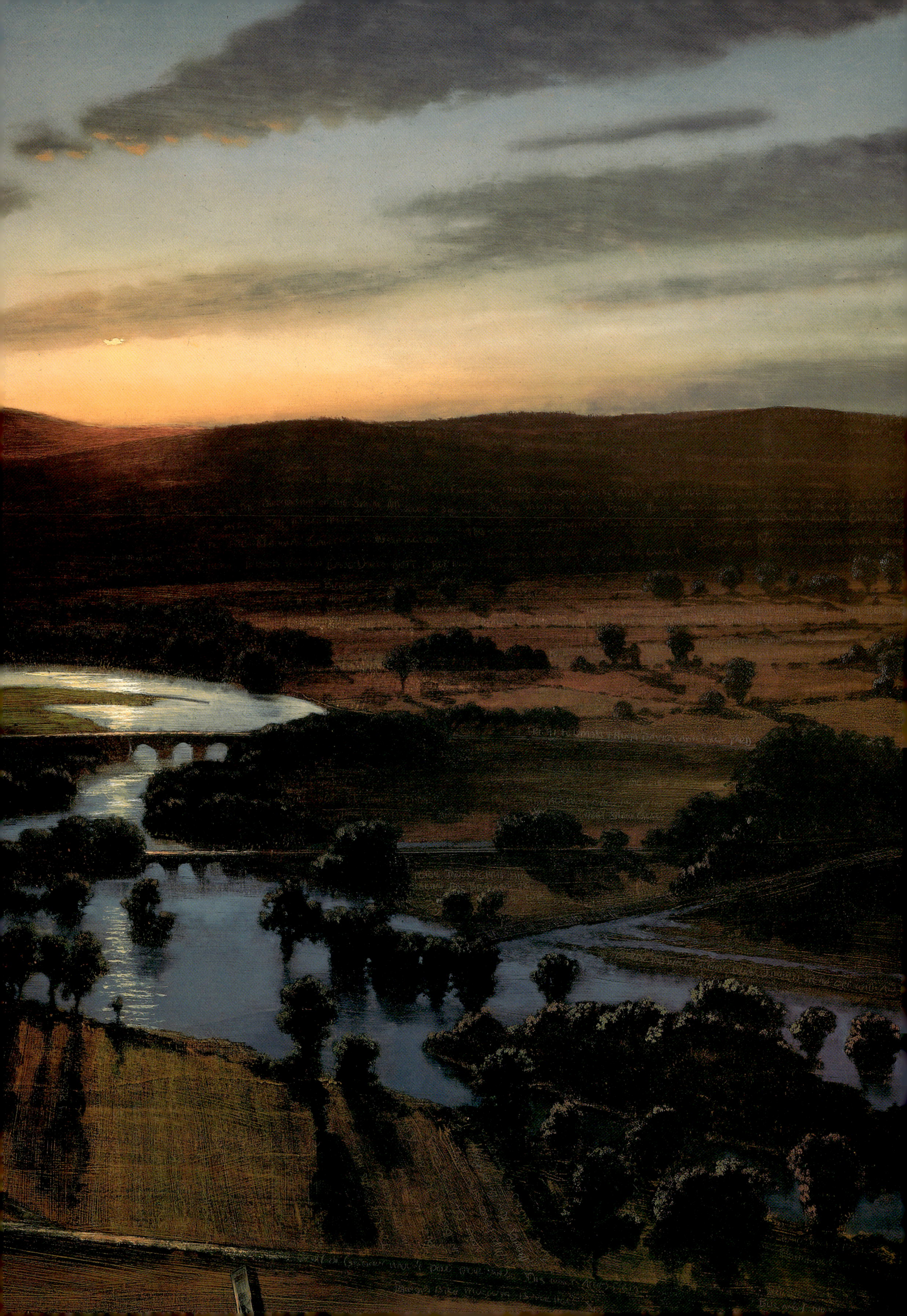

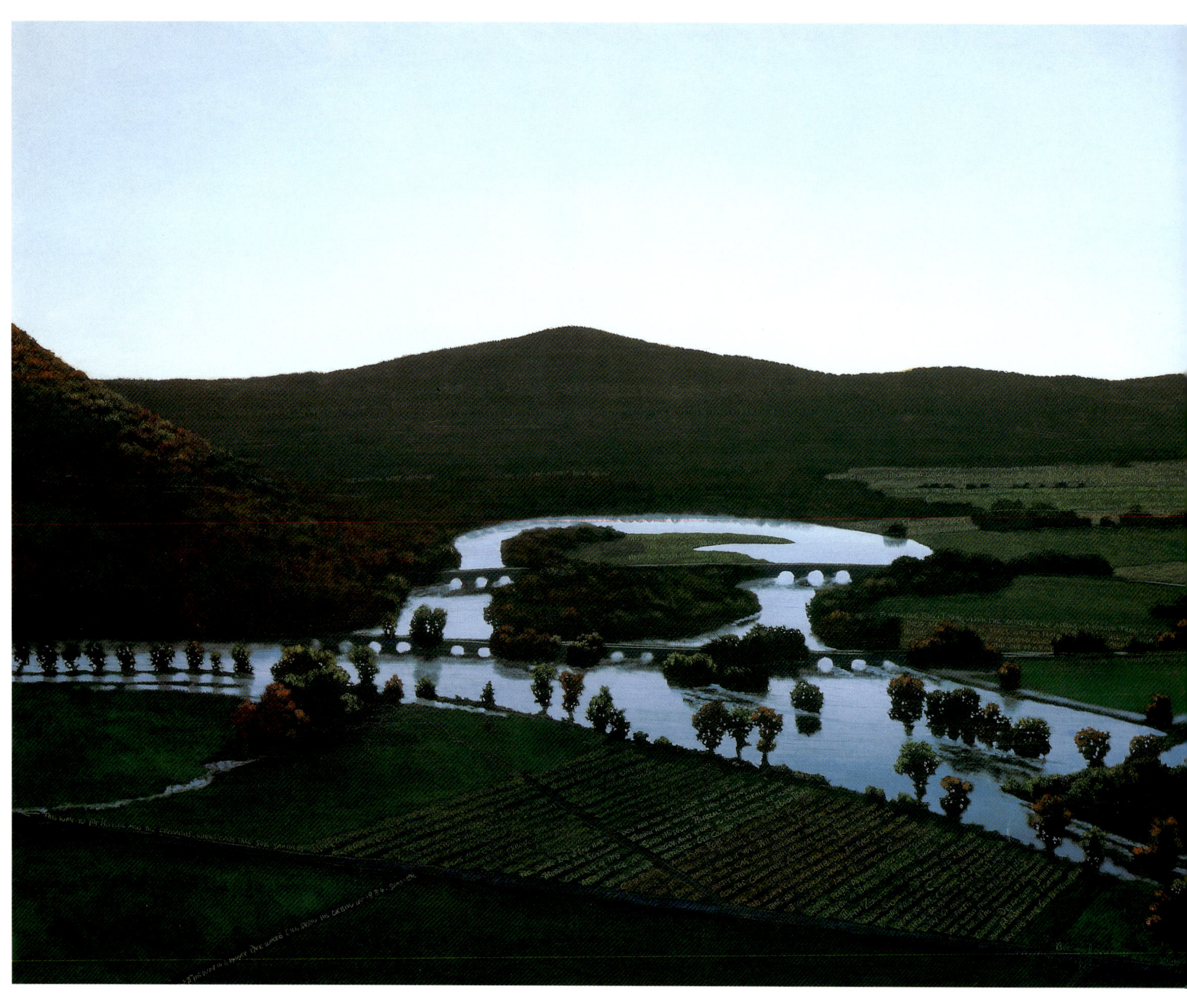

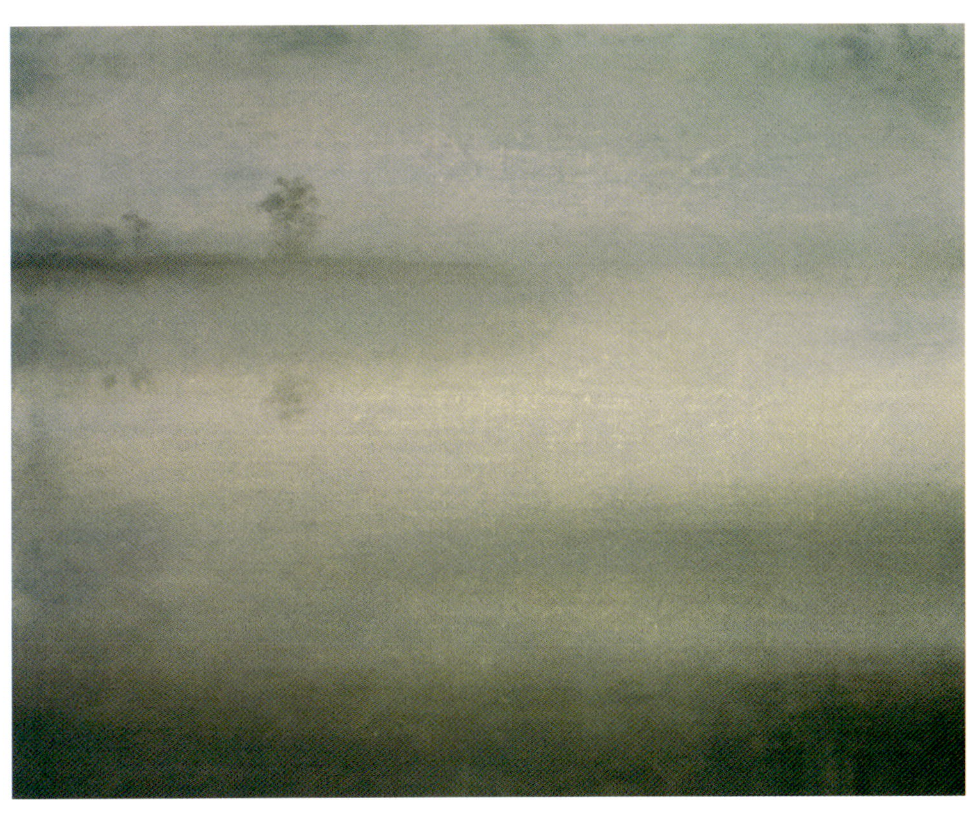

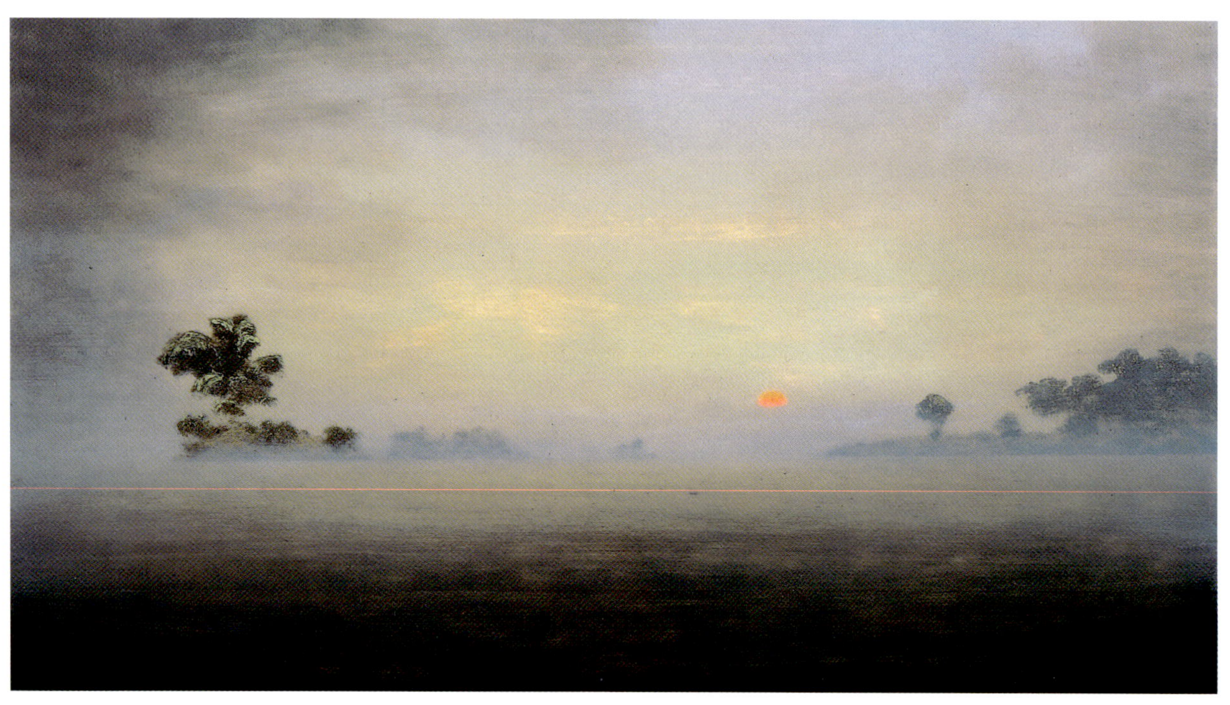

23 | 24

25 | 26

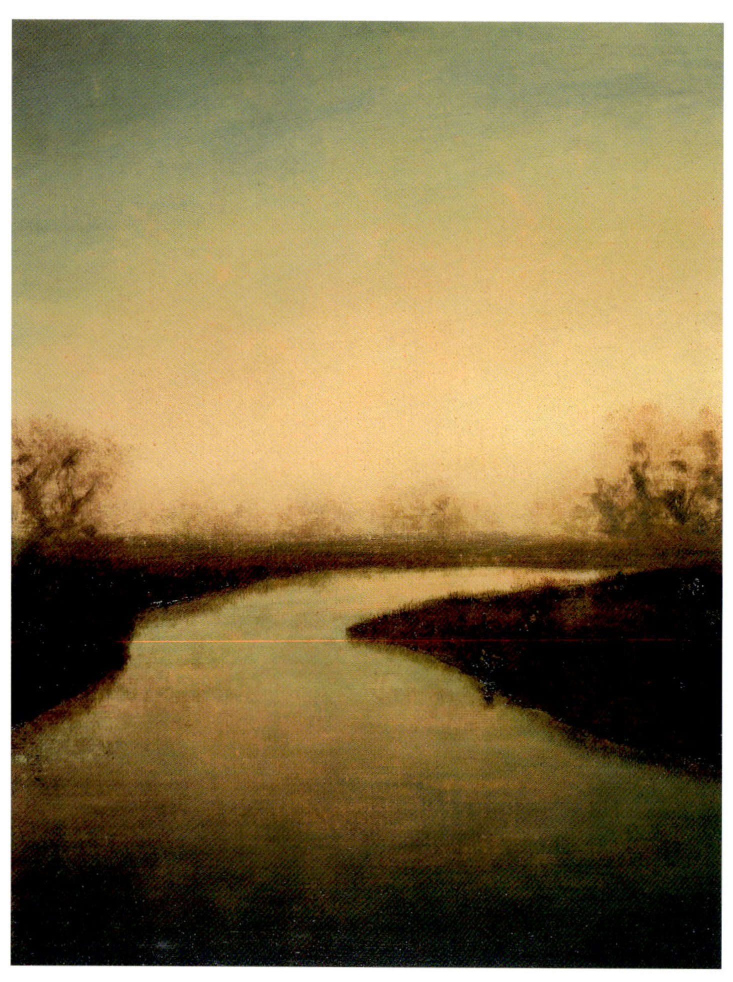

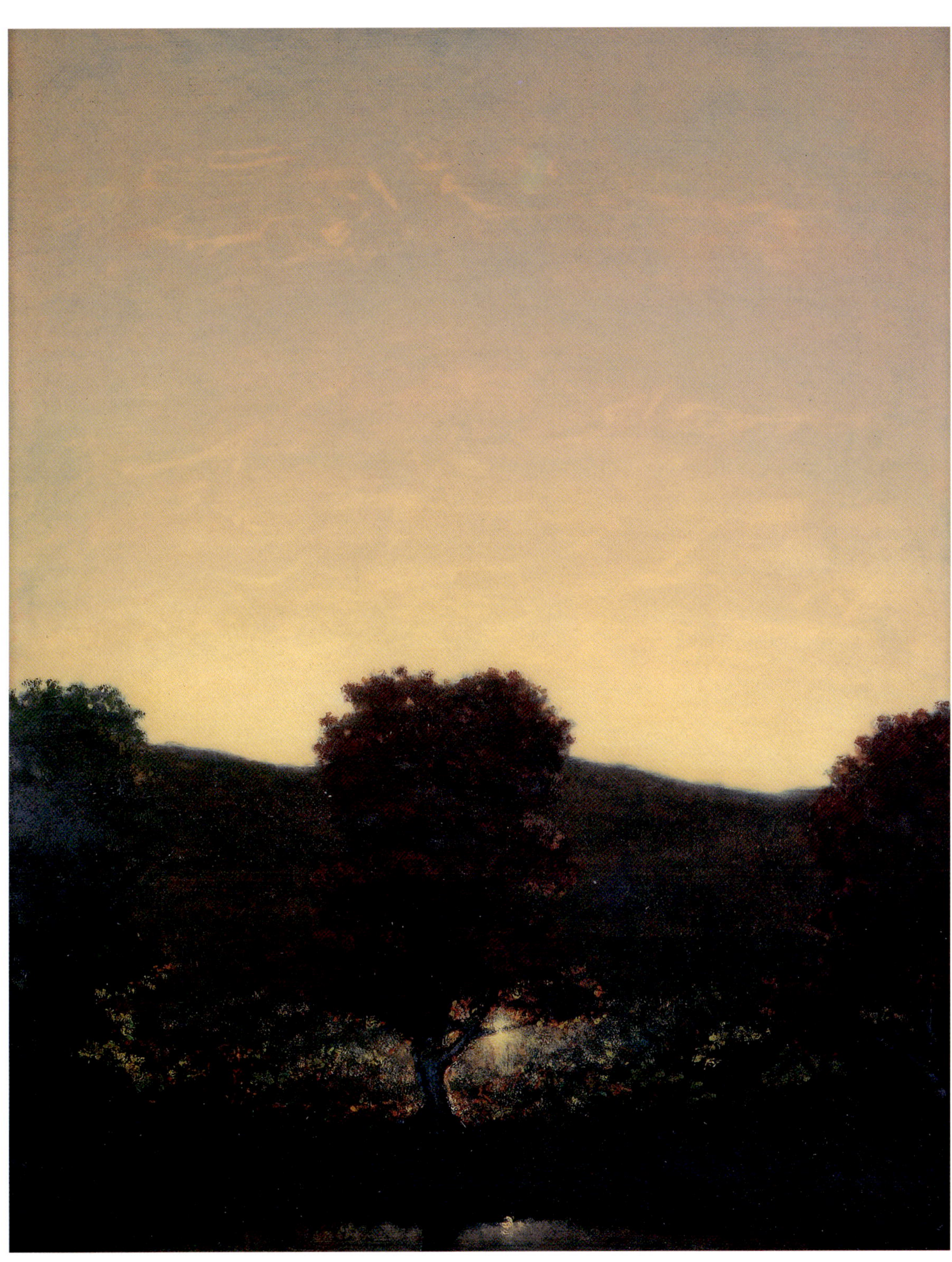

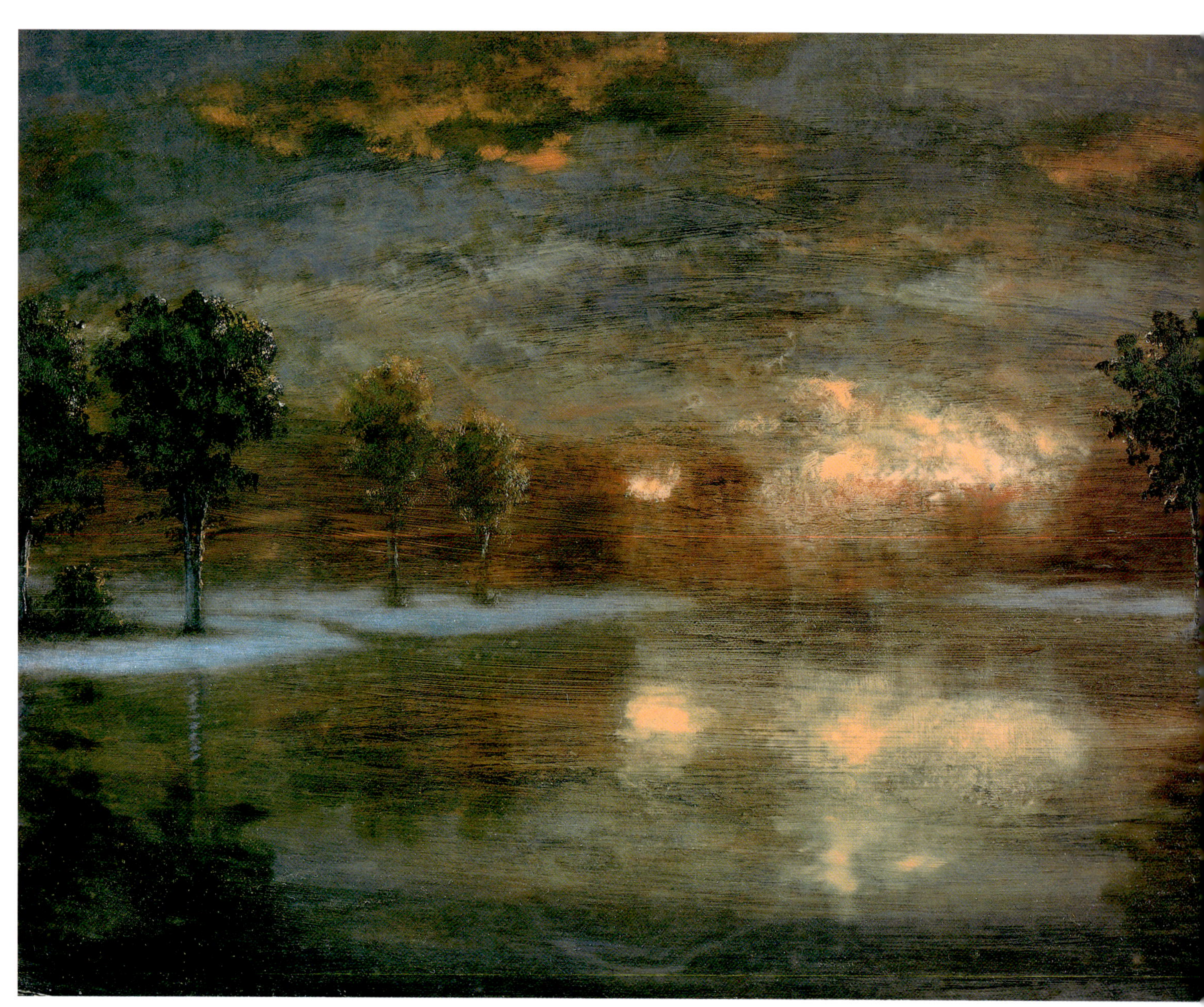

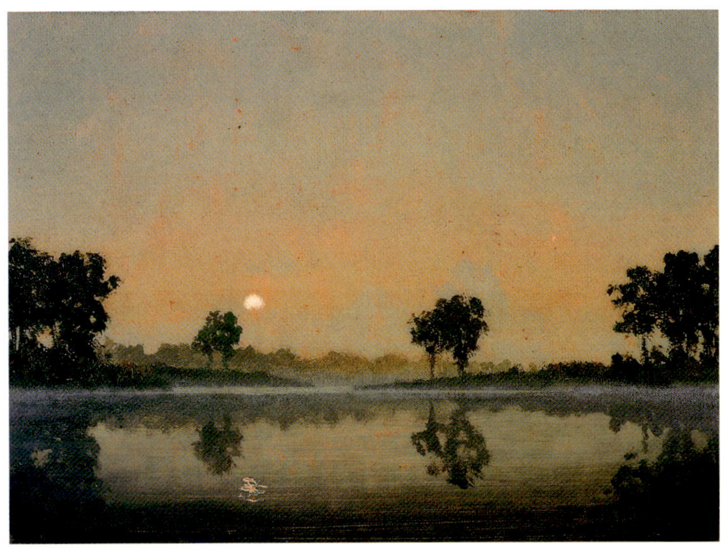

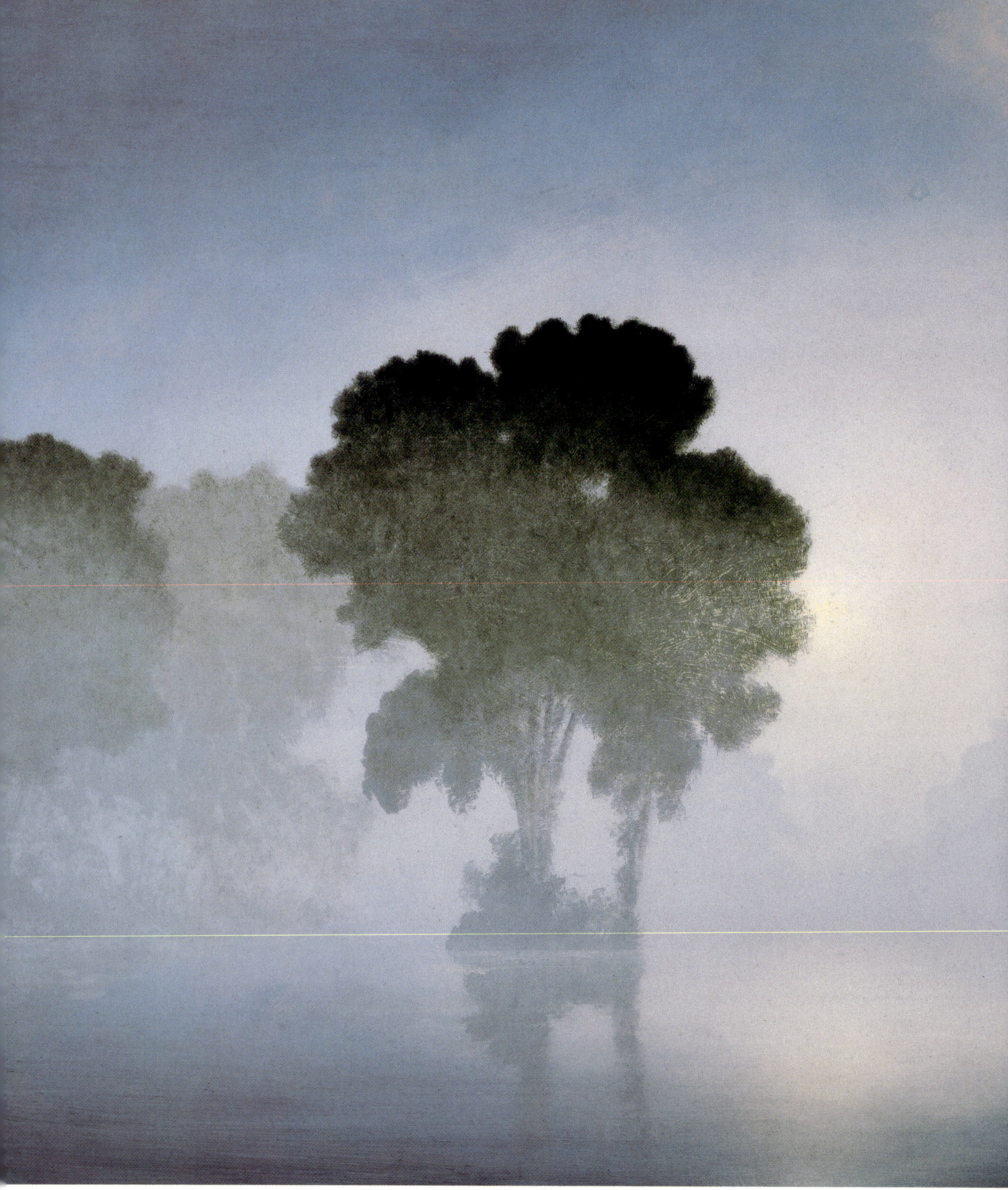

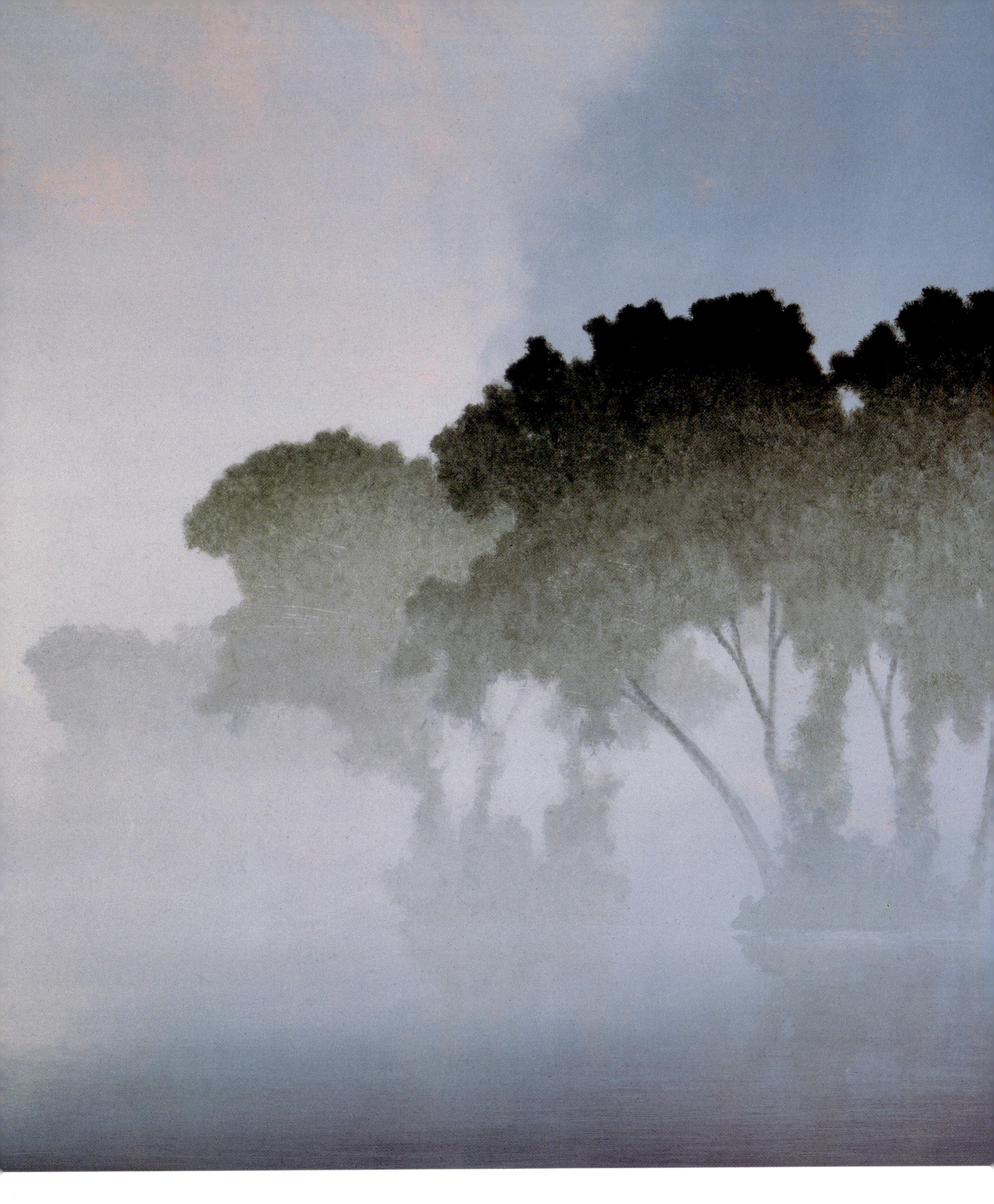

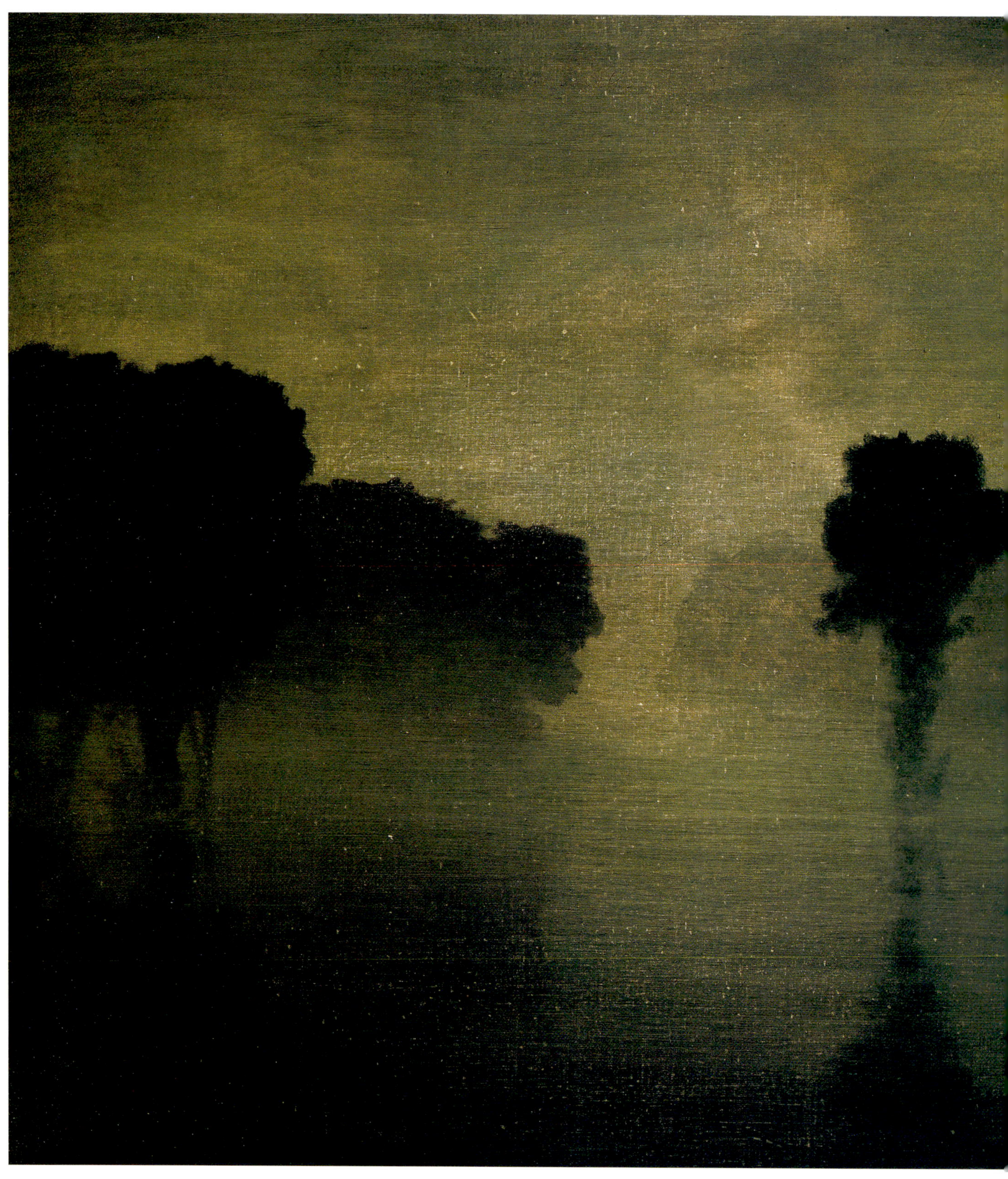

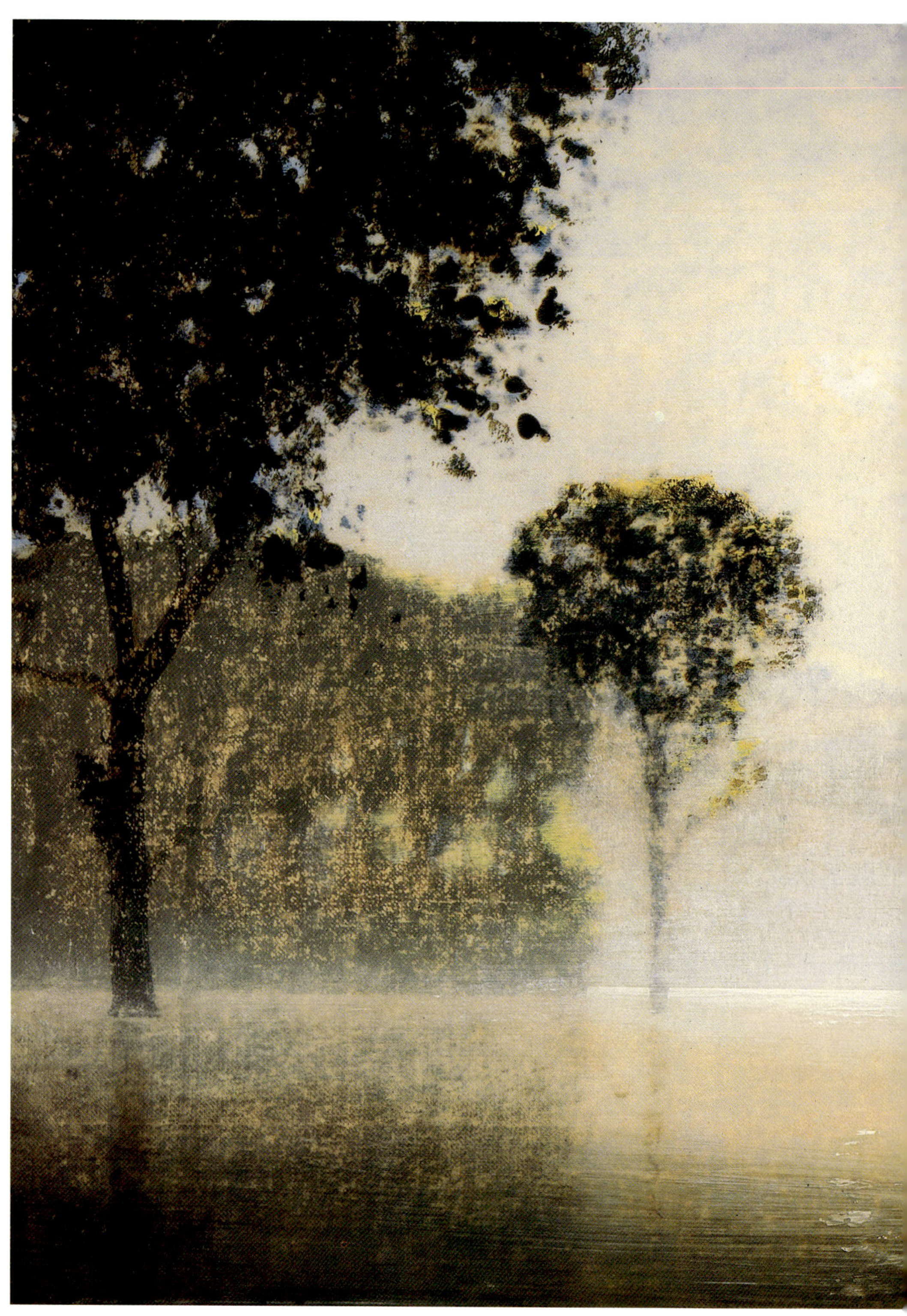

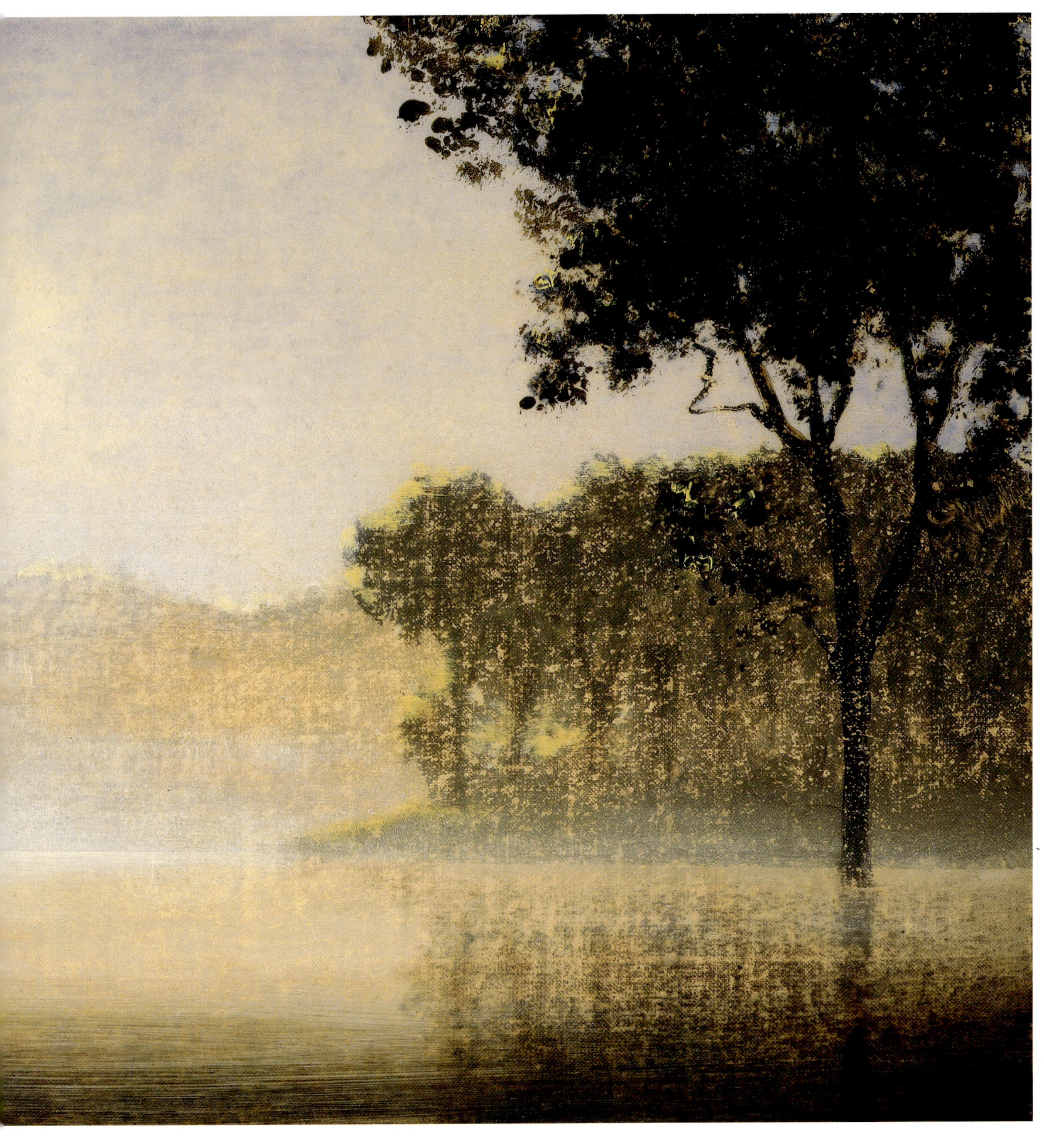

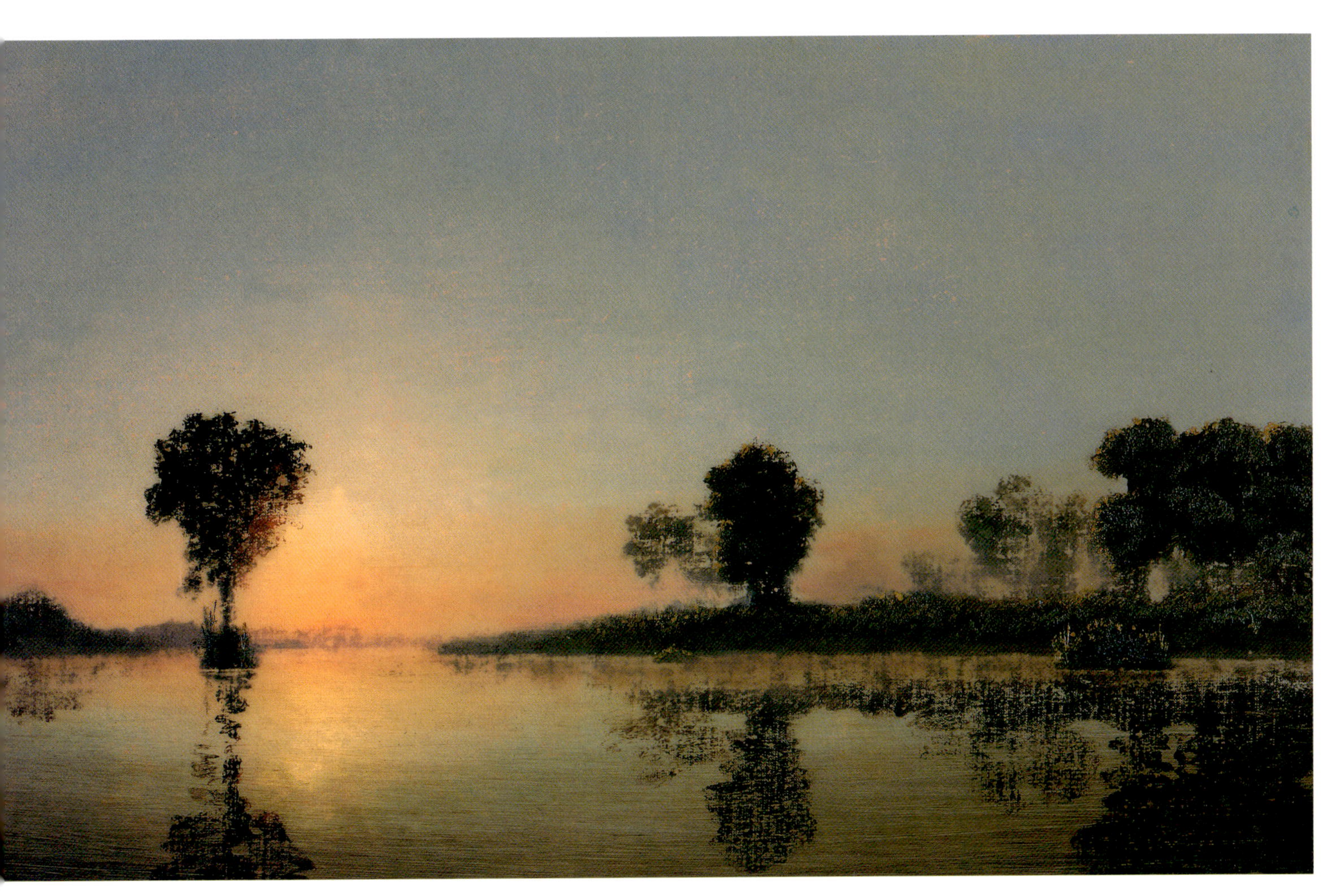

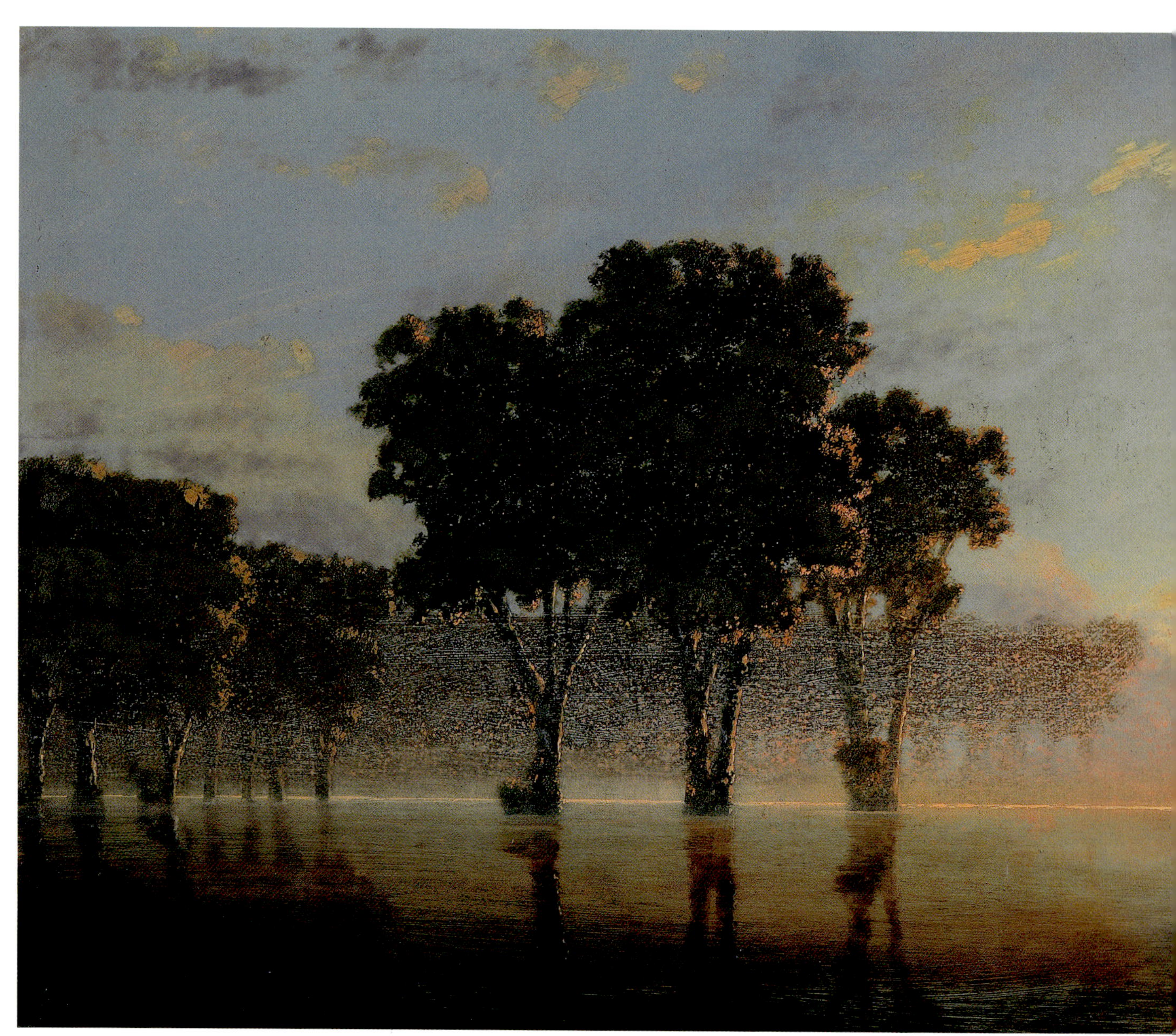

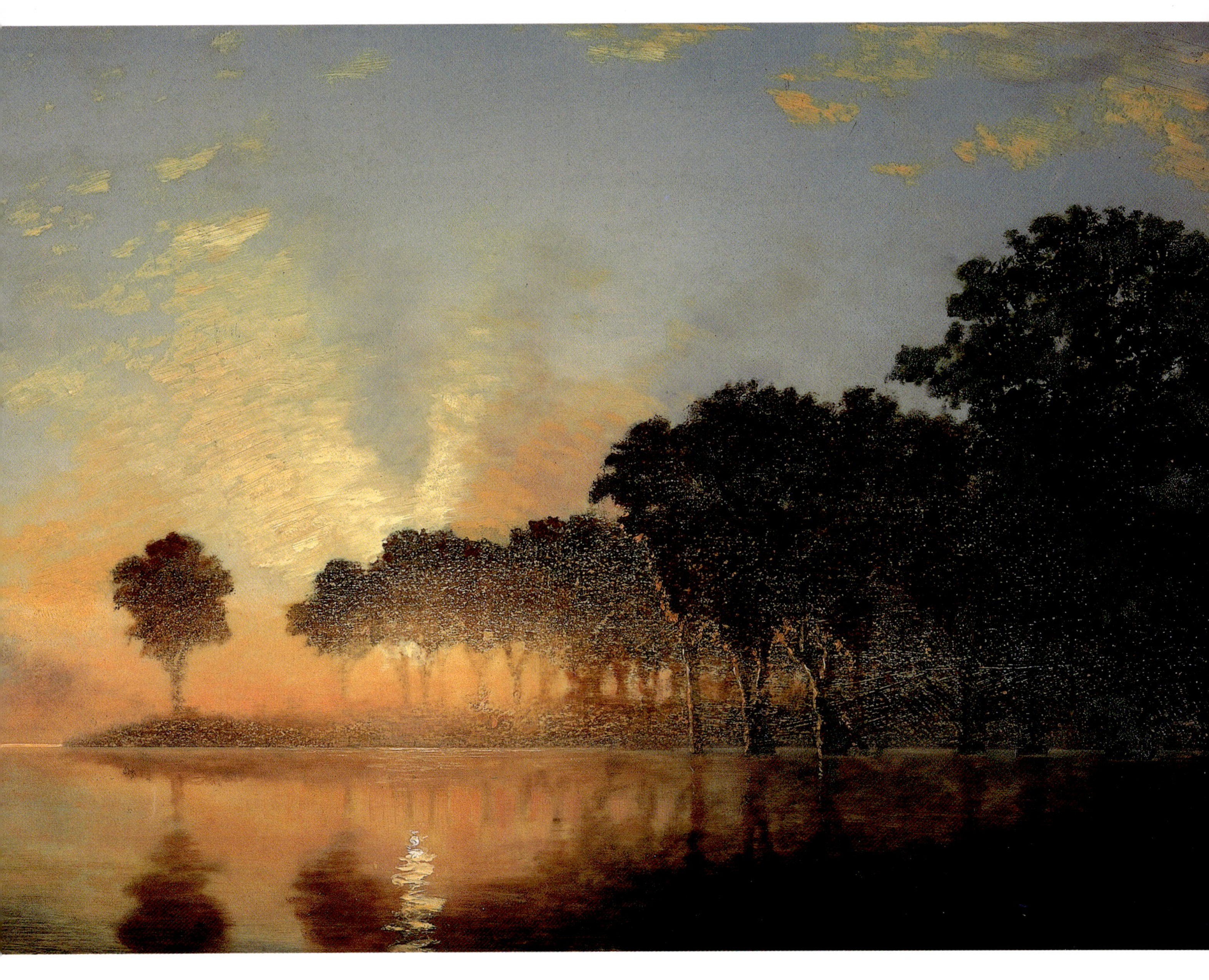

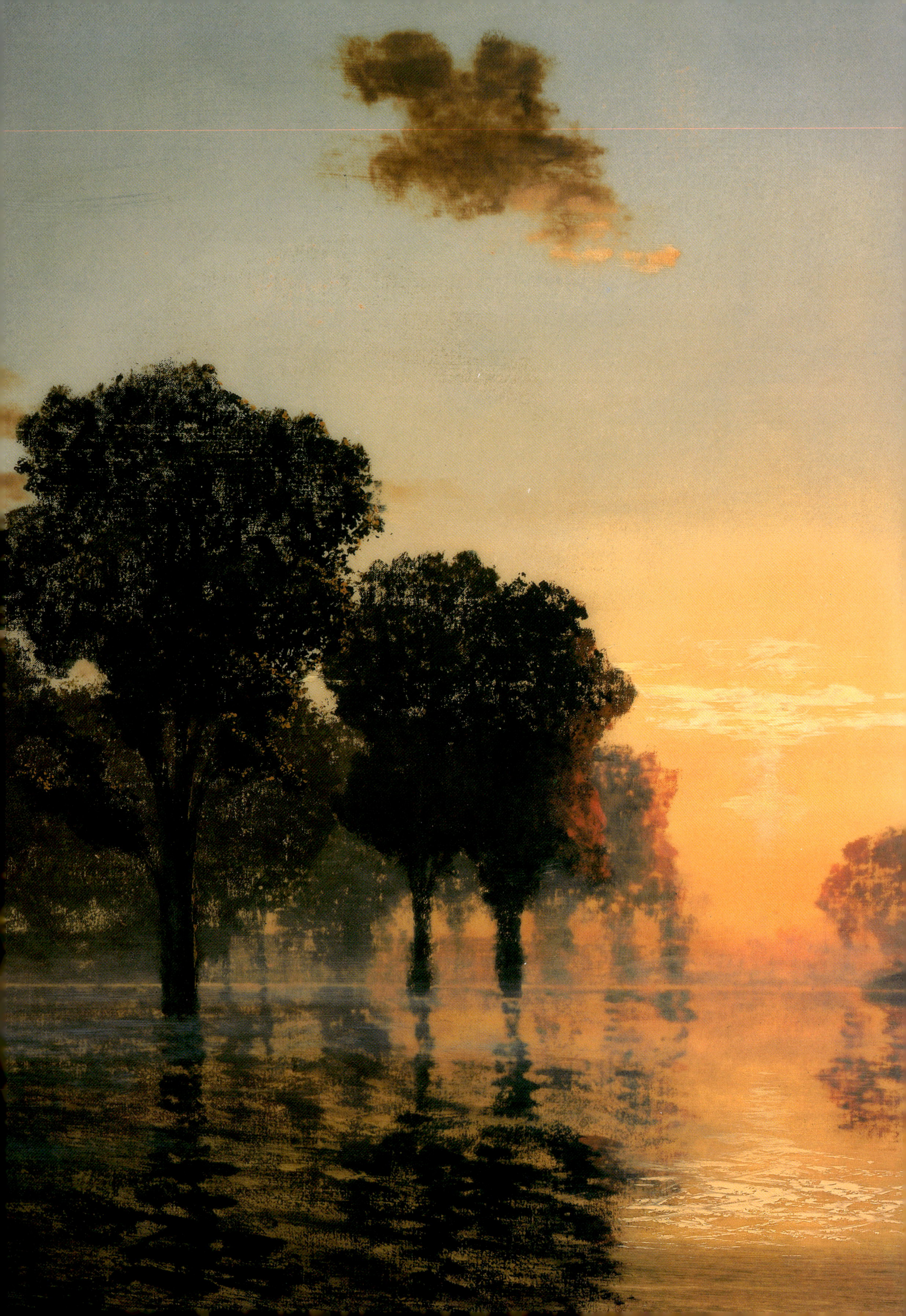

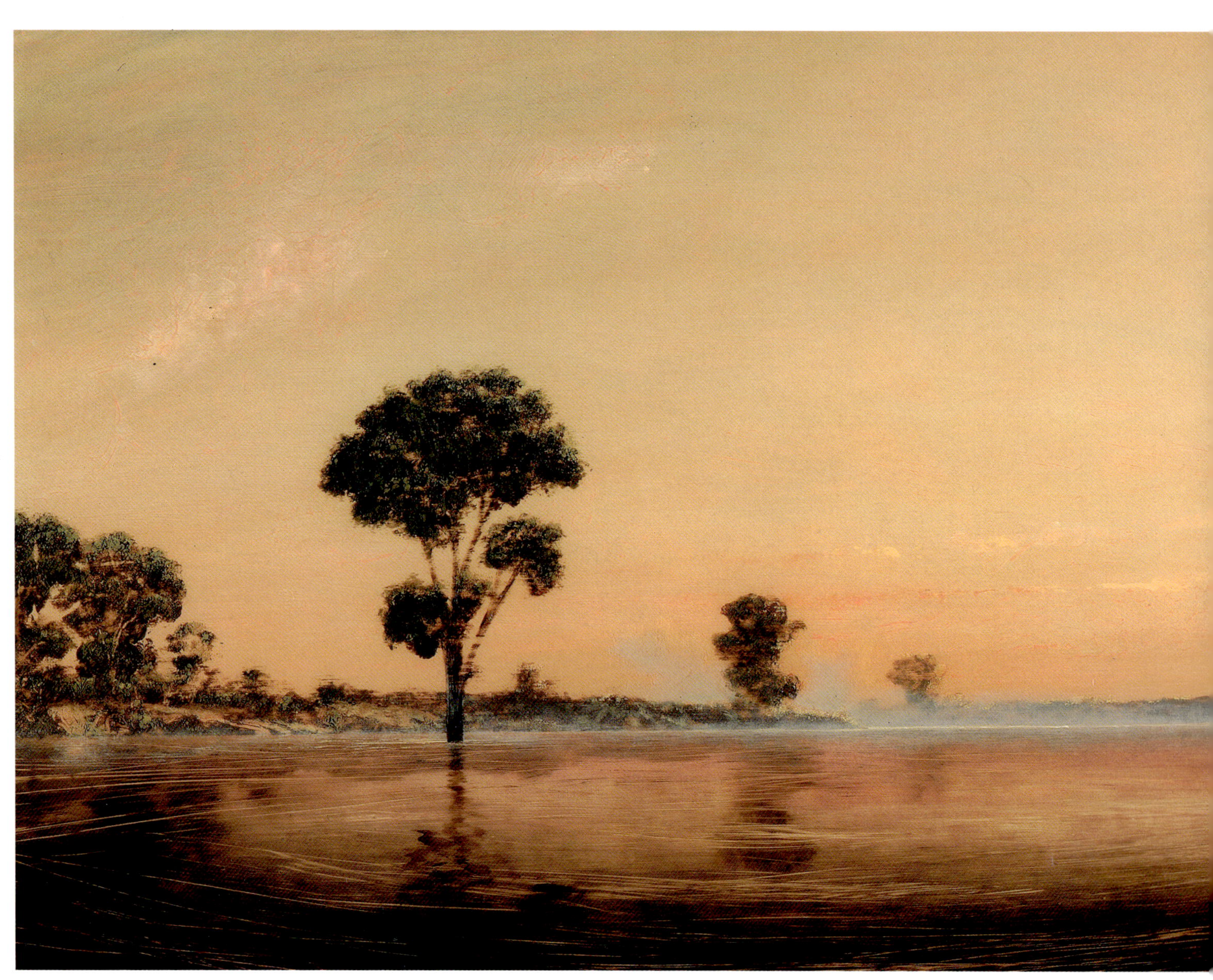

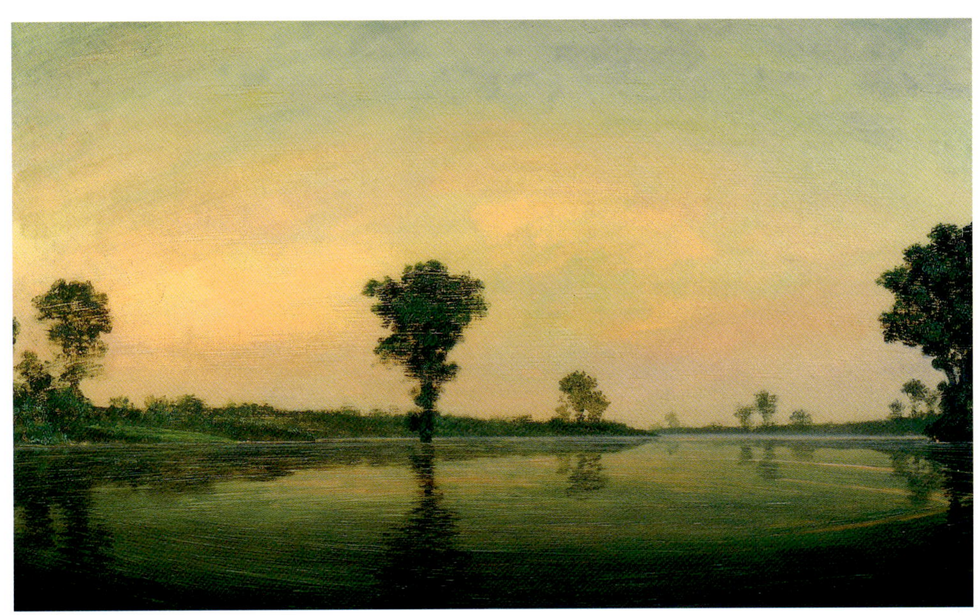

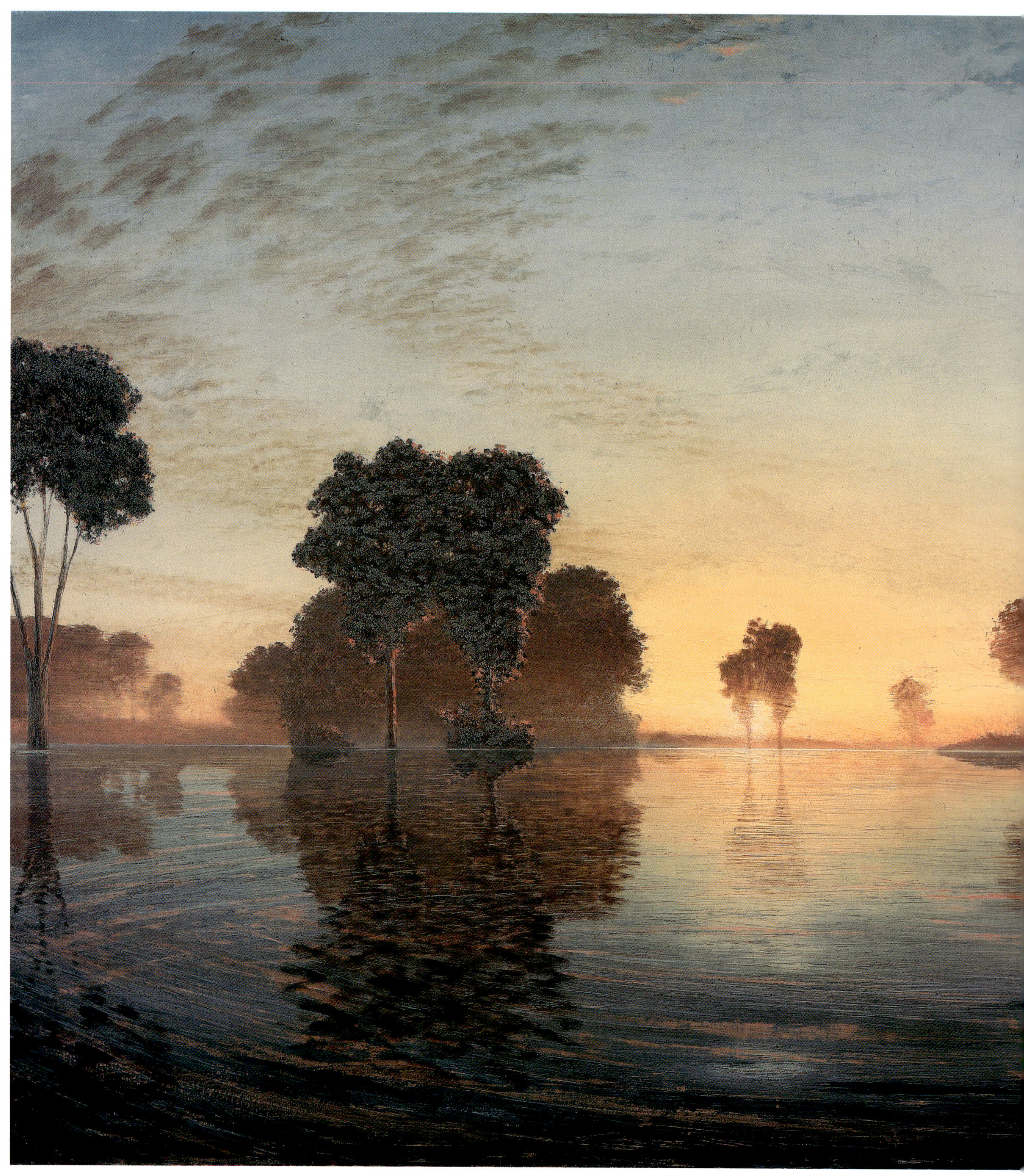

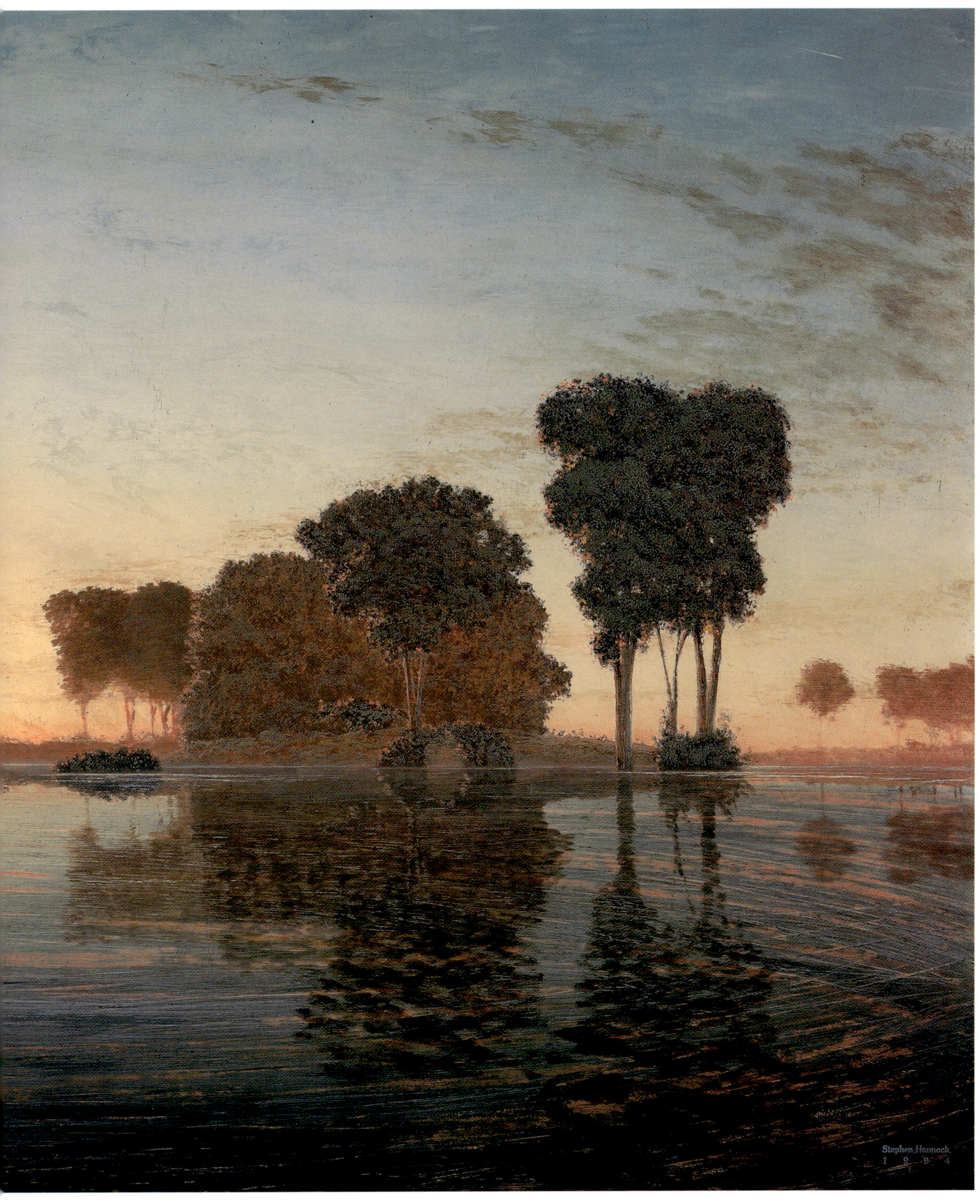
Stephen Hannock
1 9 9 4

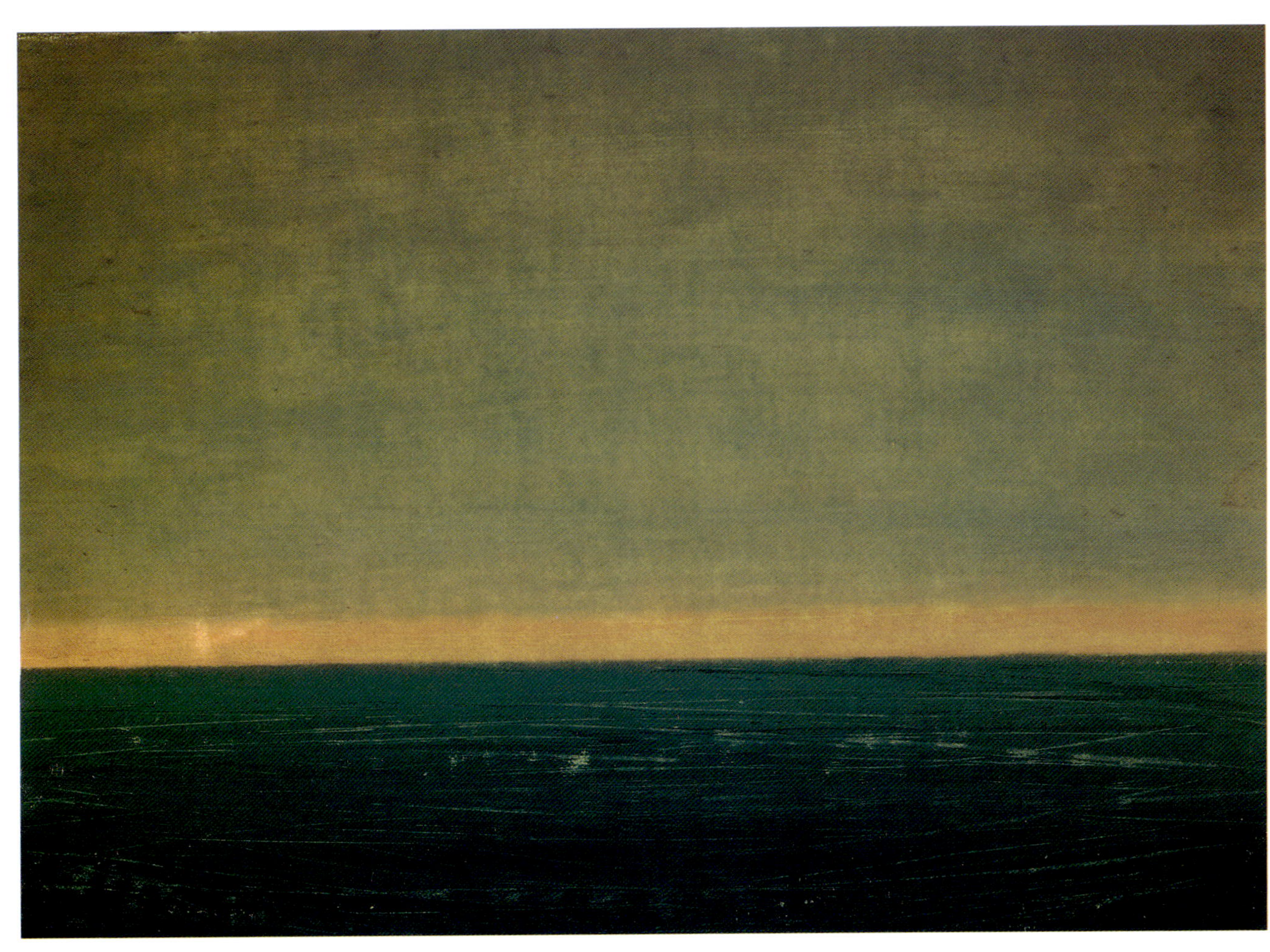

43 | 44

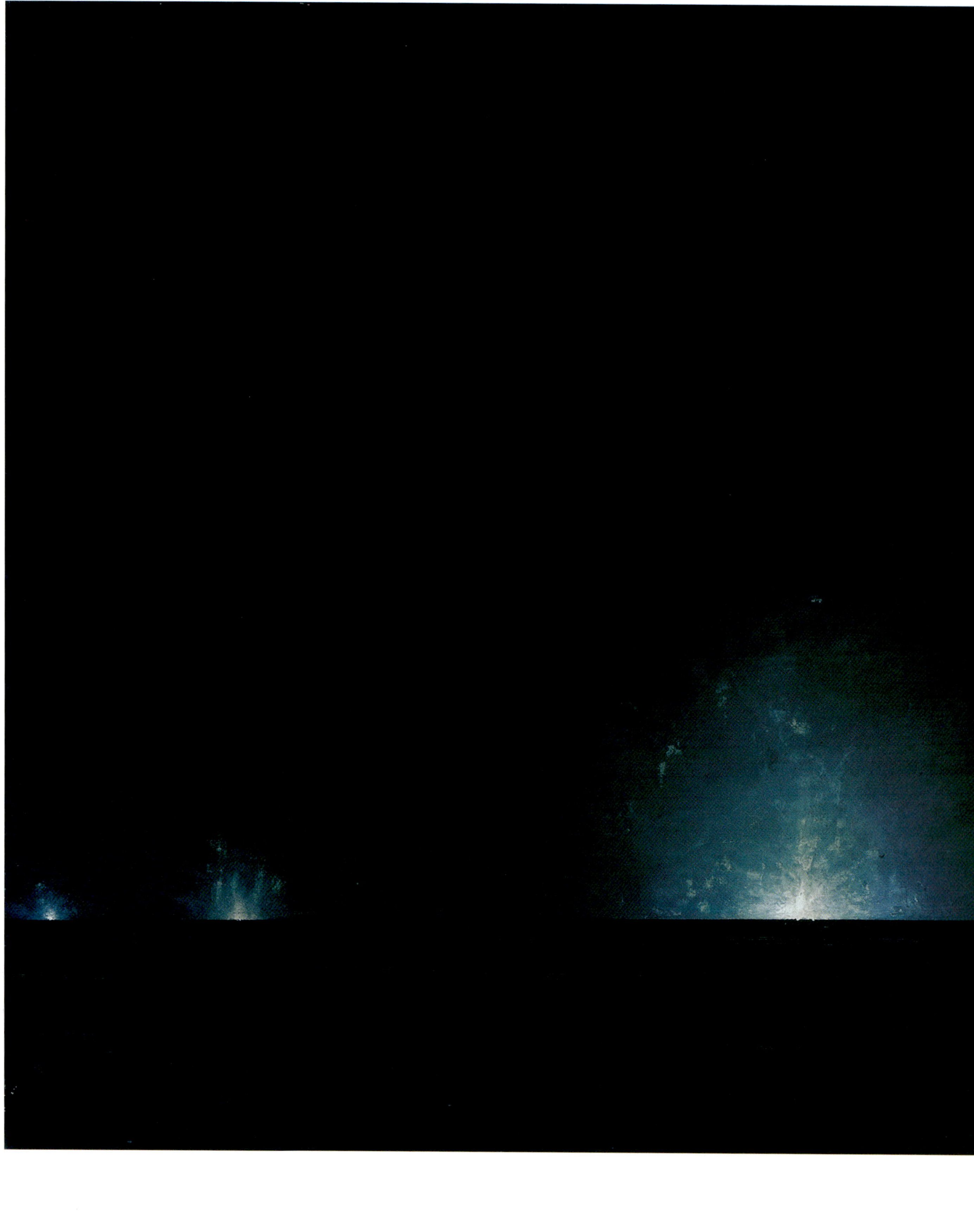

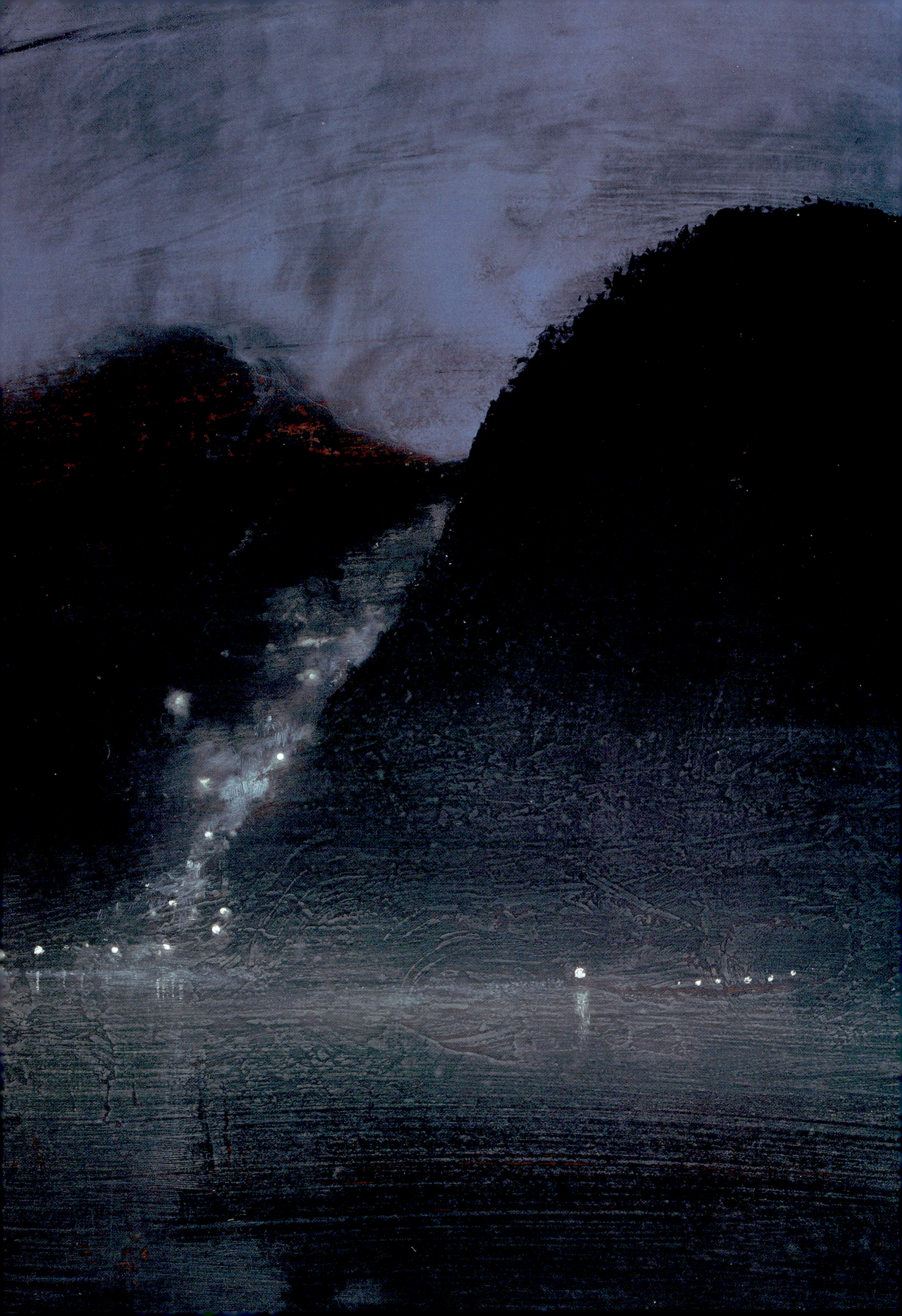

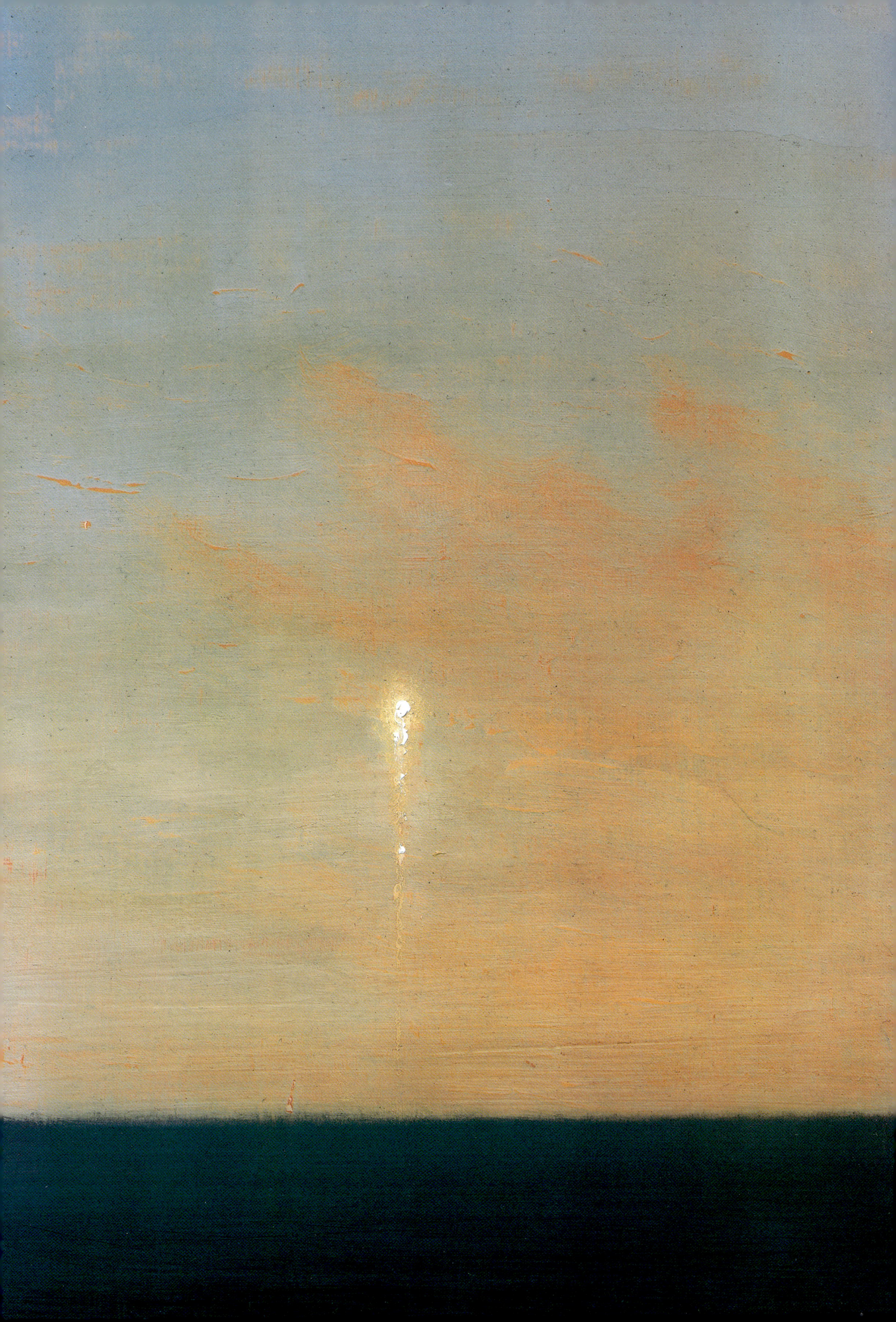

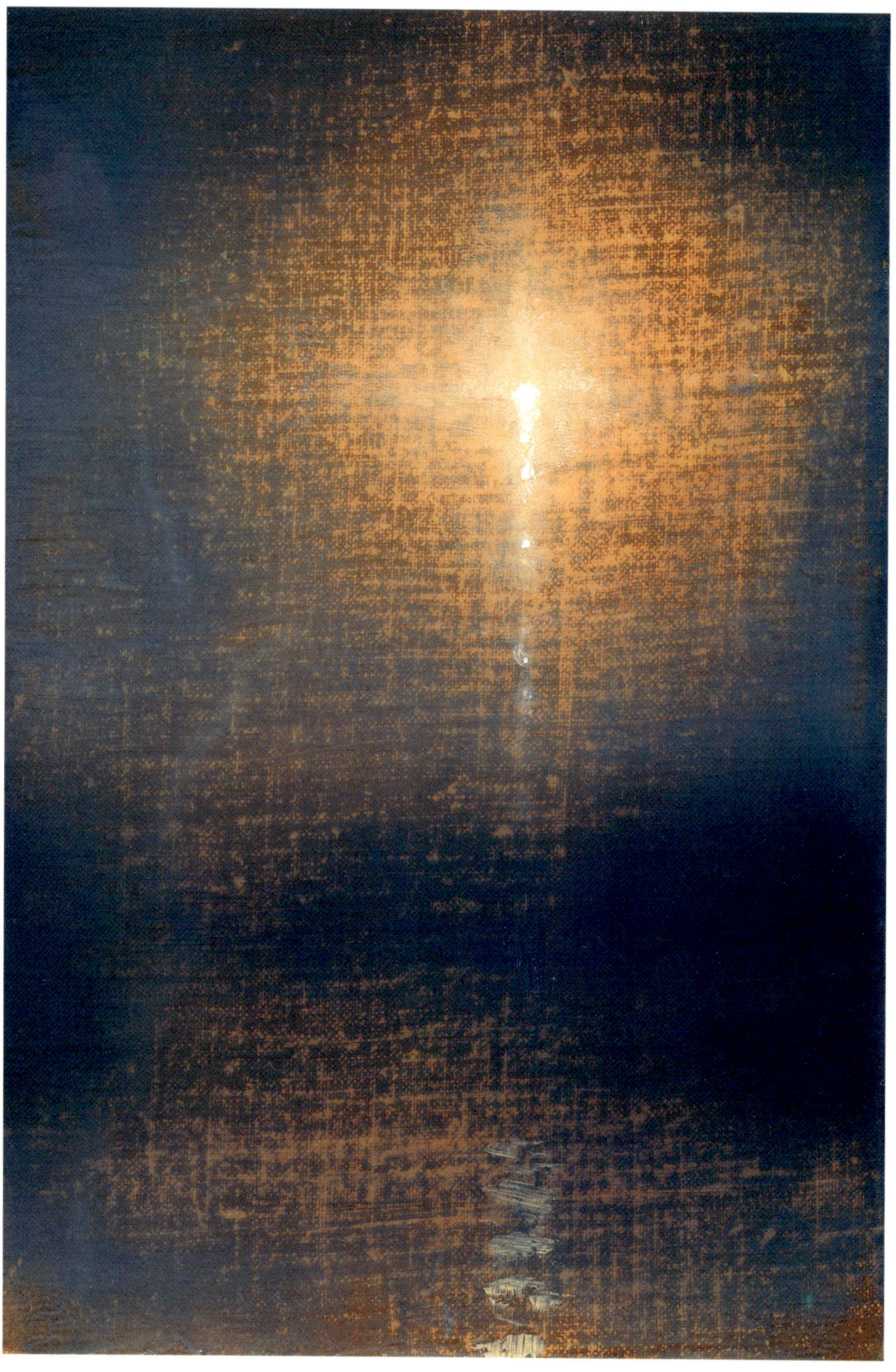

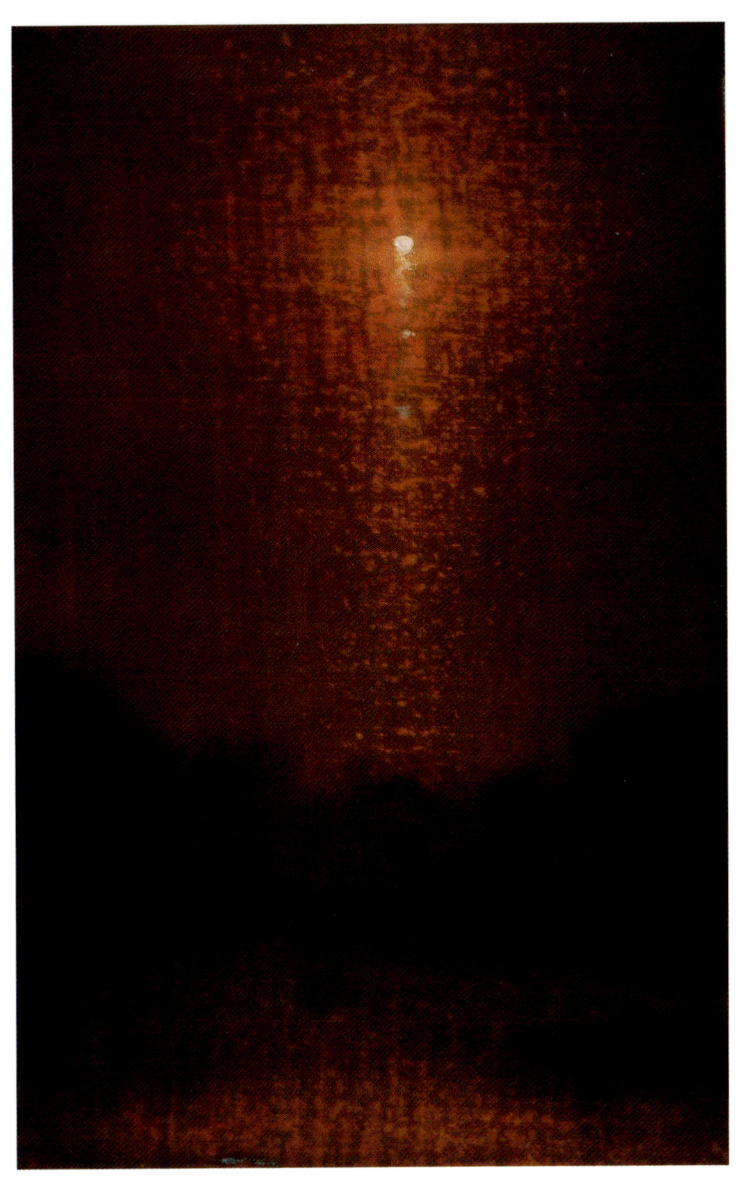

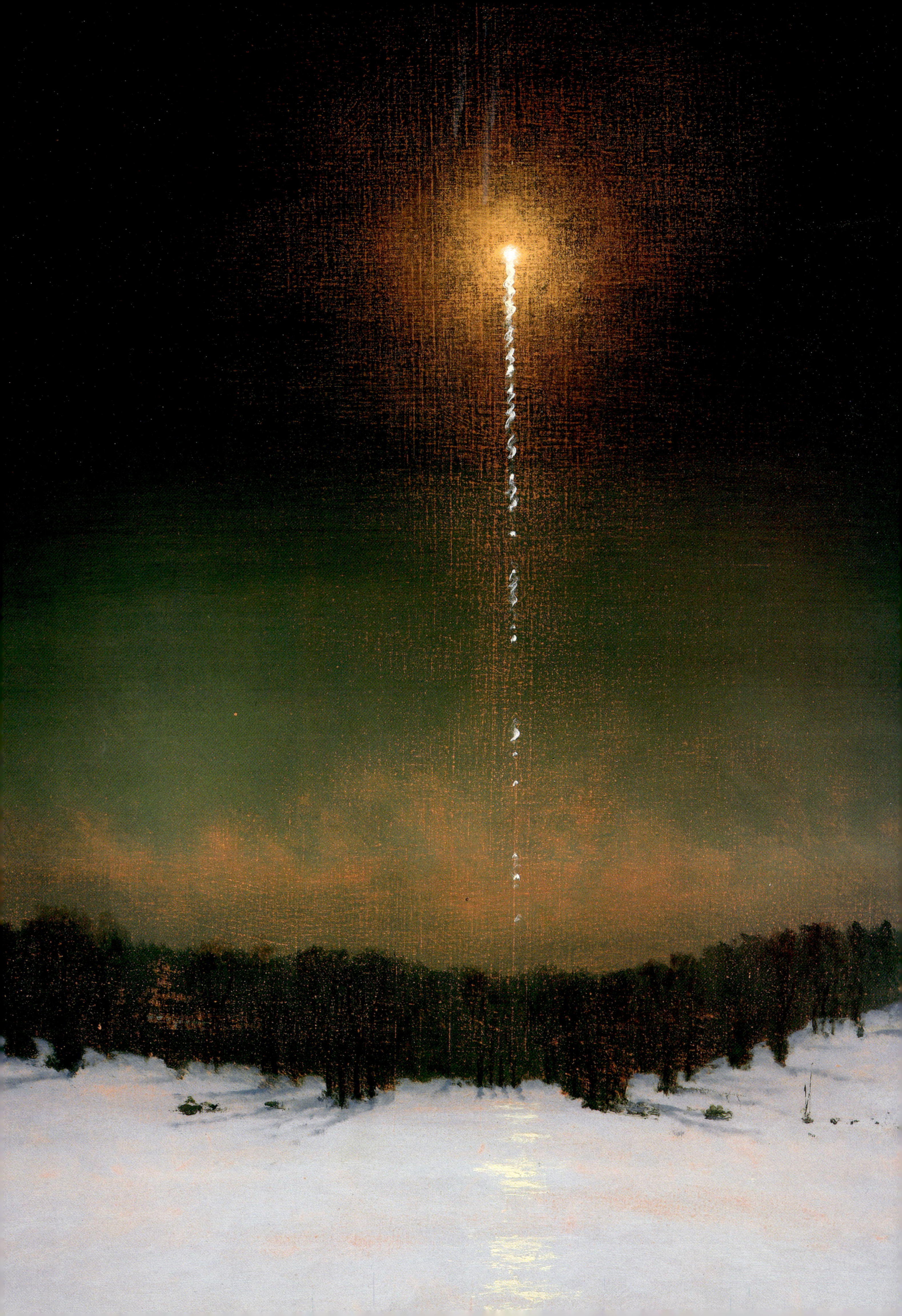

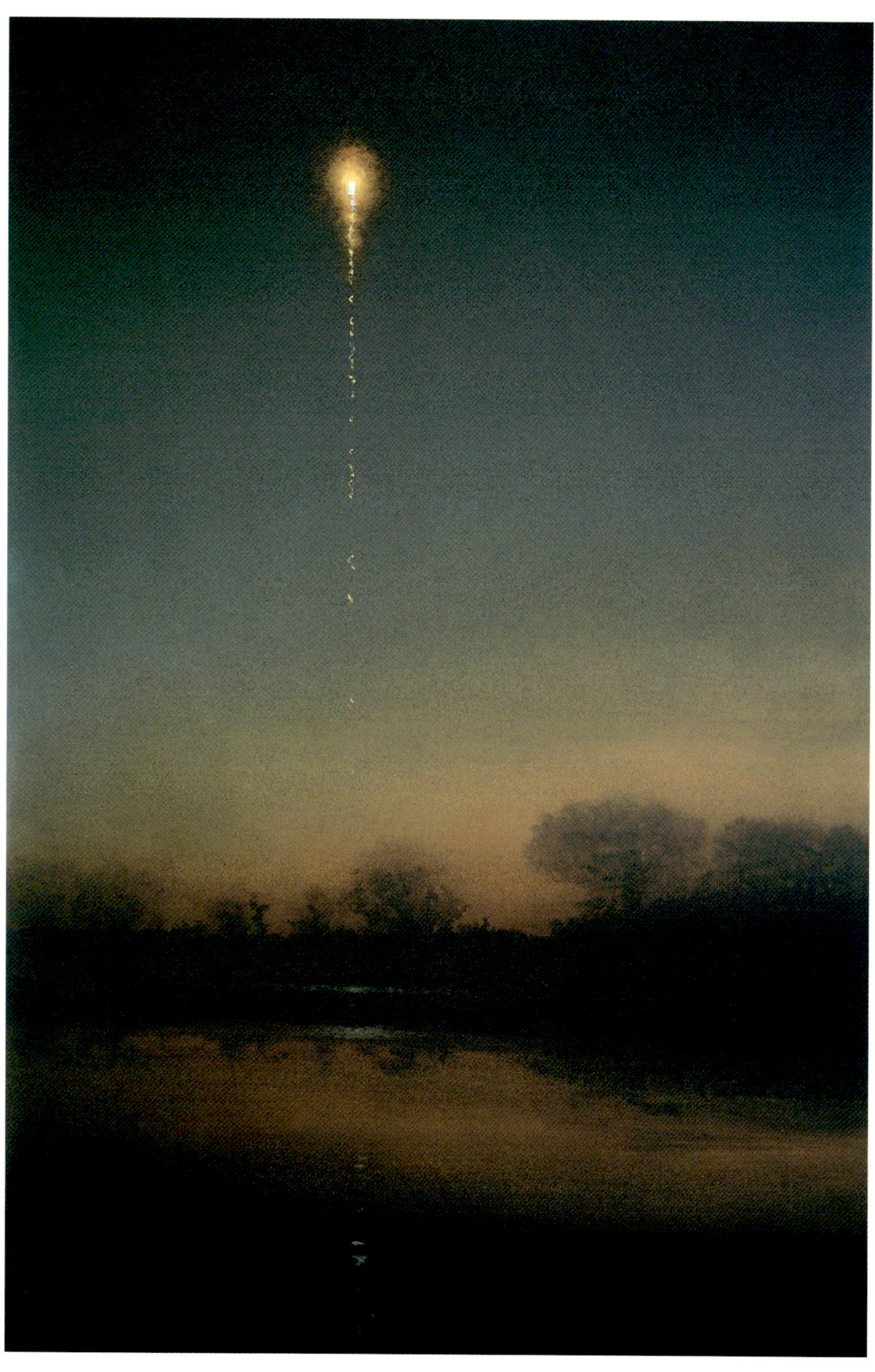

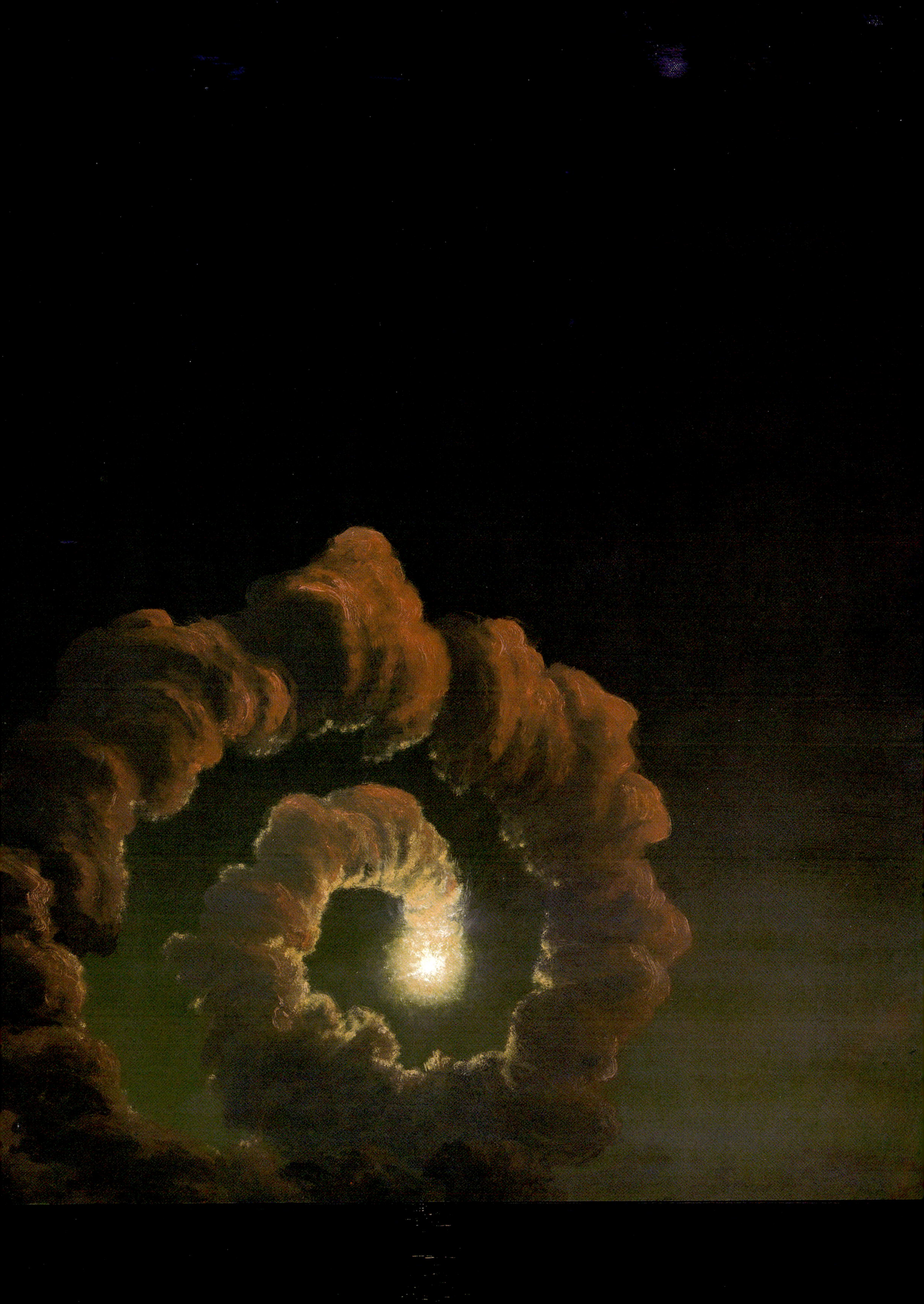

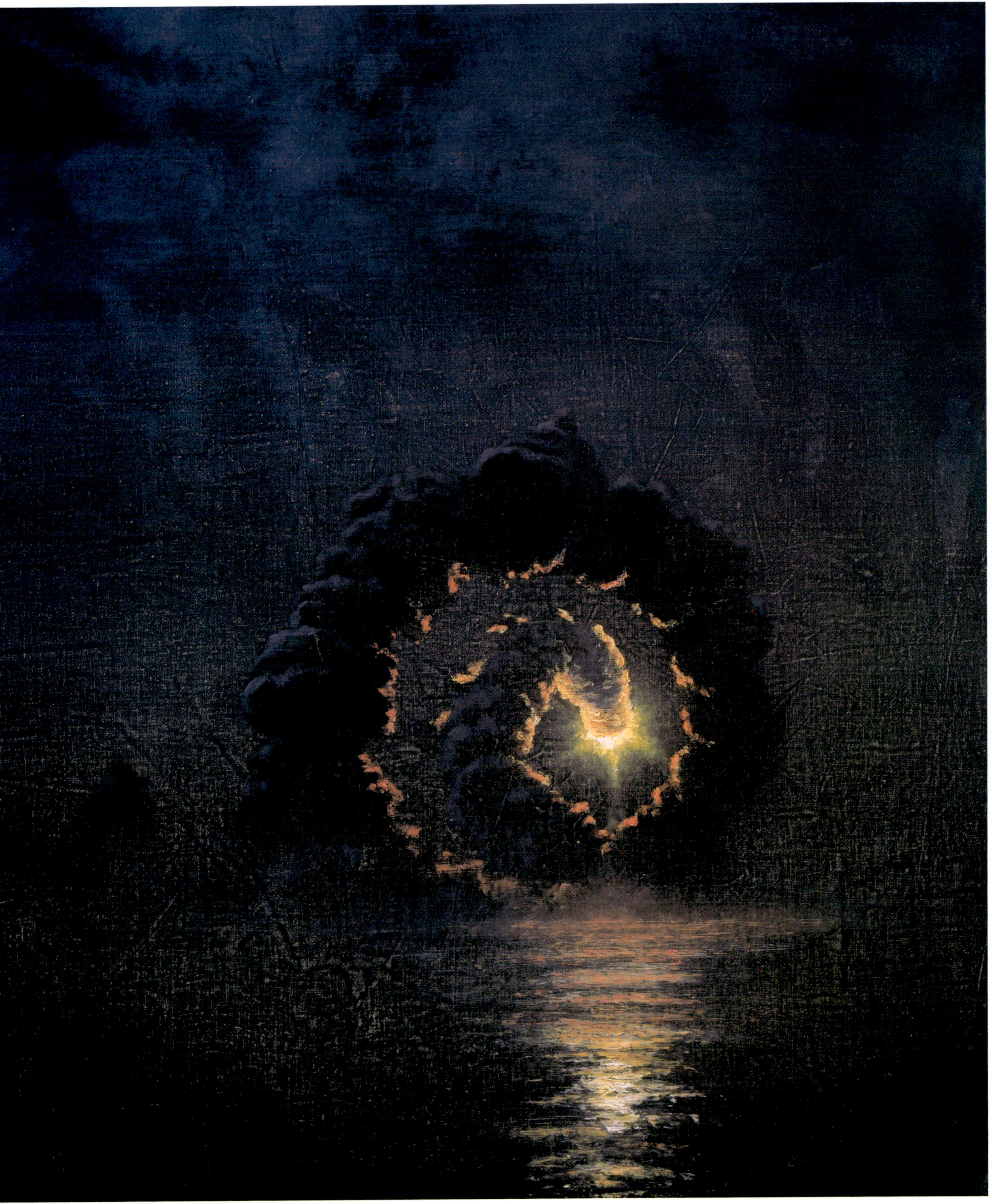

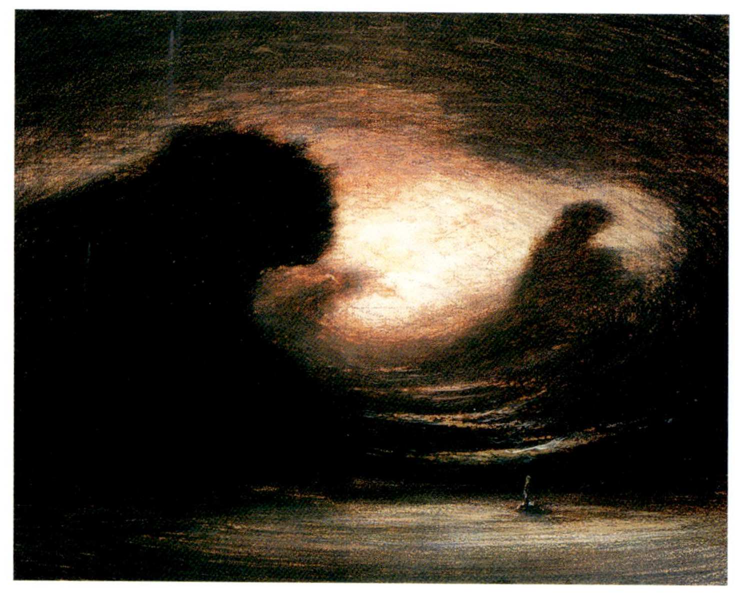

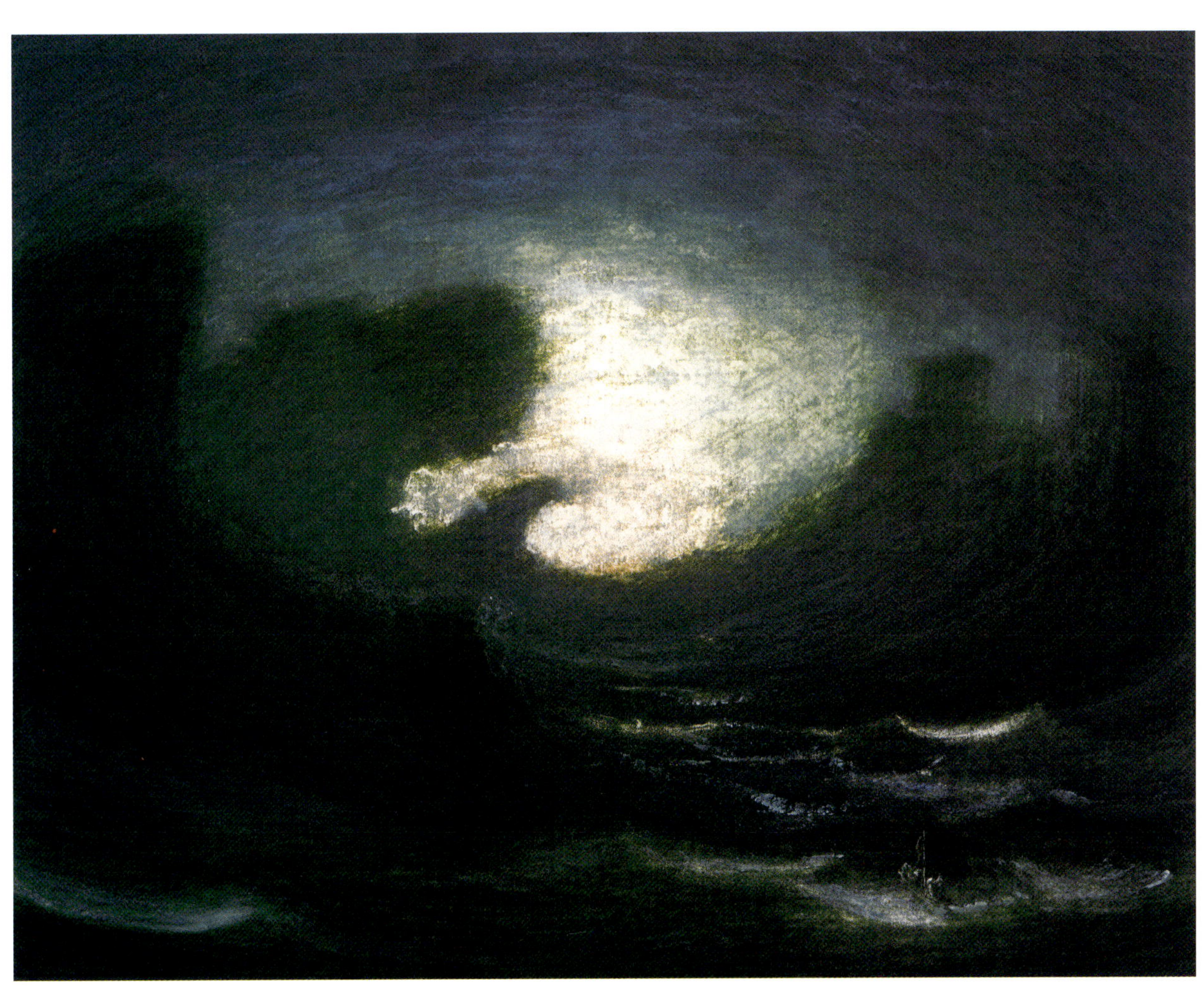

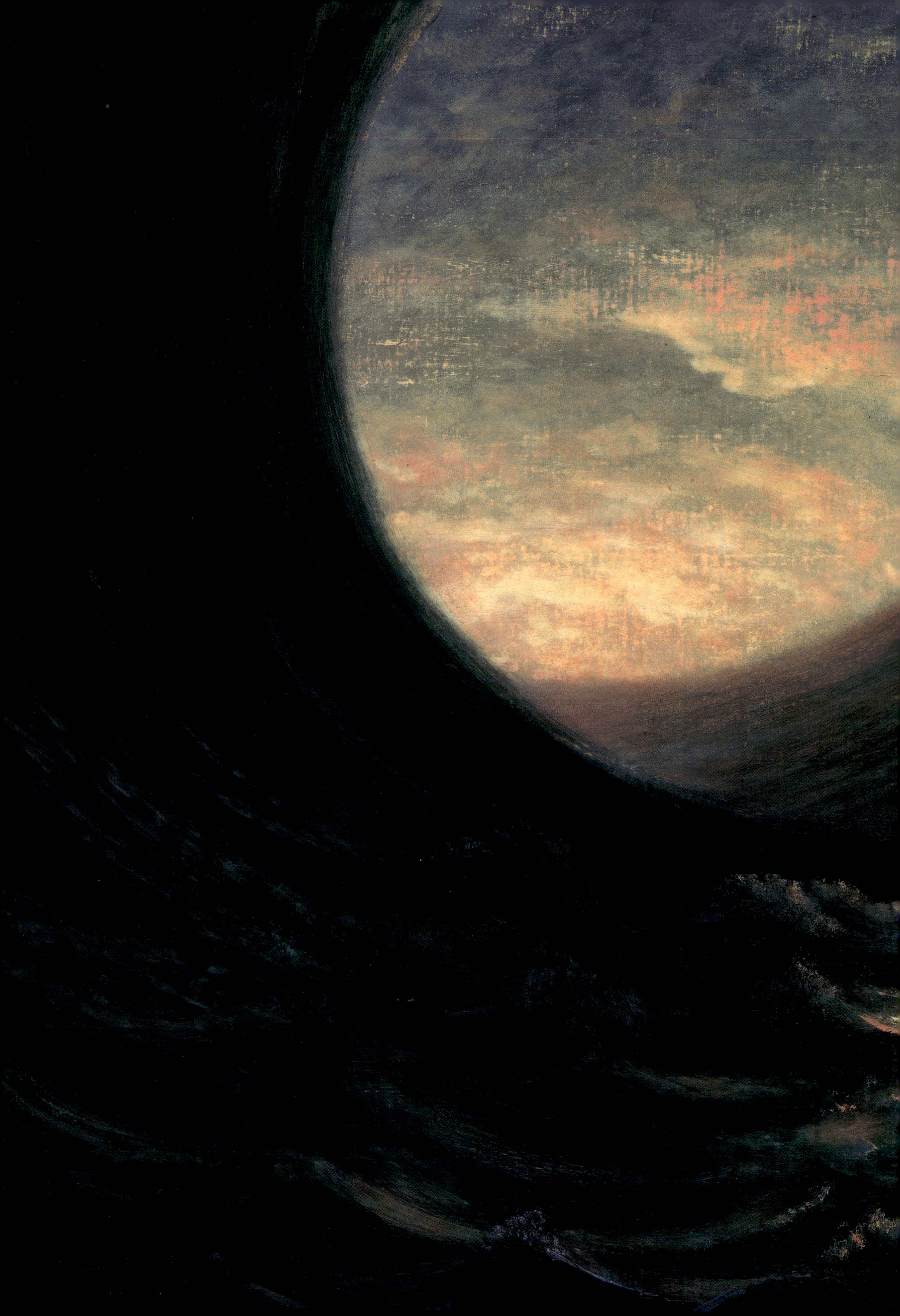

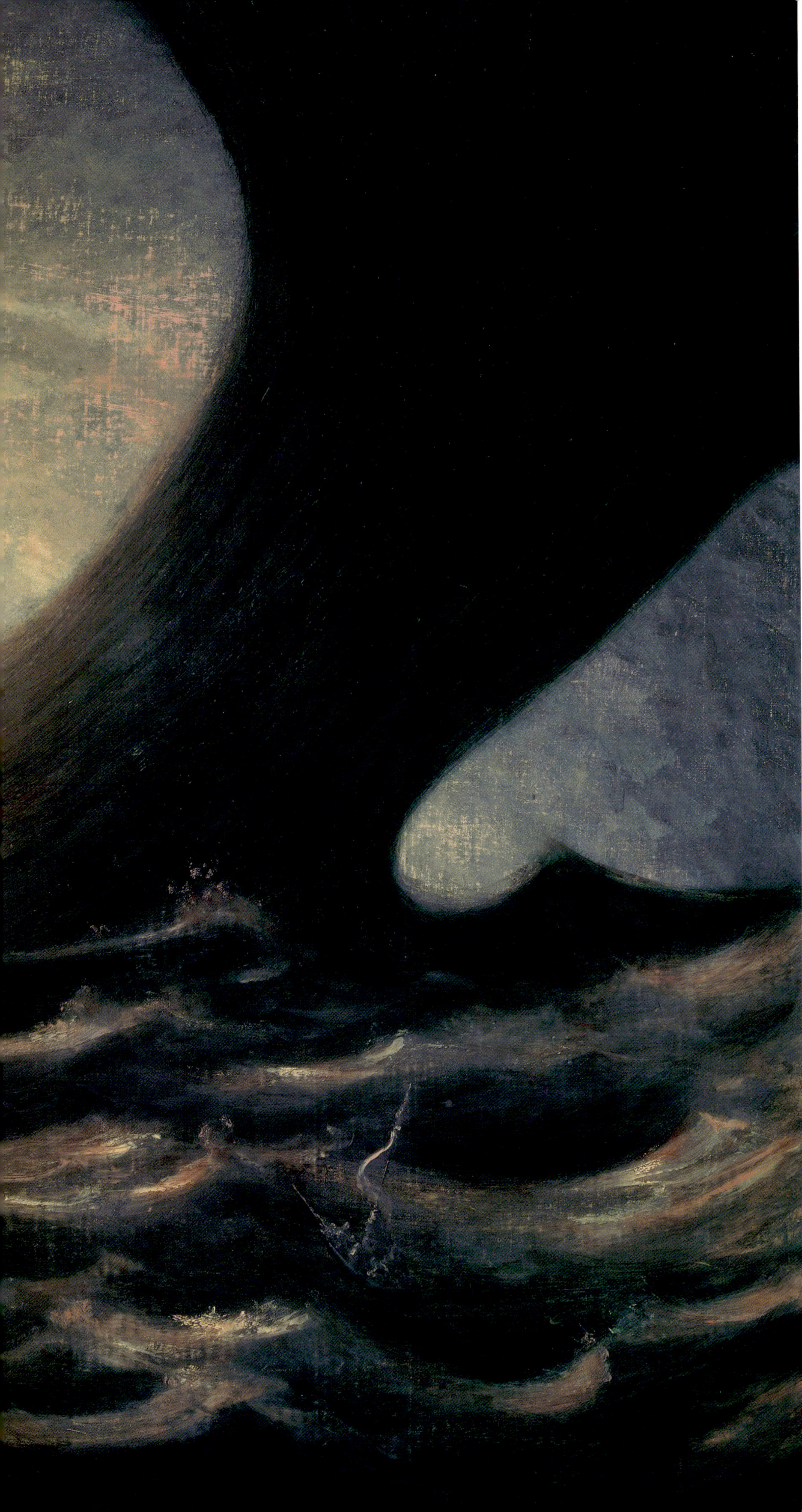

PLATE INFORMATION

1 ***New England City (Northampton, Massachusetts)***, 1983
Polished oil on canvas
72 x 54 in.
Private collection

2 ***Flooded River with Three Sisters***, 1990
Polished oil on canvas
48 x 108 in.
Private collection

3 ***Montana Nocturne with Crazy Mountain***, 1994
Polished oil on canvas
10 x 18 in.
Private collection

4 ***Napa Dawn, Autumn Light***, 1997
Polished oil on canvas
22½ x 50 in.
Private collection

5 ***Napa Dawn, Spring Light***, 1997
Polished oil on canvas
42 x 84 in.
Private collection

6 ***Dusty Dusk in Tuscany***, 1996
Polished oil on canvas
7 x 11 in.
Private collection

7 ***Tuscan Vineyard with Storm Approaching***, 1998
Polished oil on canvas
9¾ x 7¼ in.
Private collection

8 ***Villa il Palagio: After the Storm***, 1999
Polished oil on canvas
7 x 8½ in.
Private collection

9 ***Tuscan Tapestry at the Close of the Day***, 1996
Polished oil on canvas
5½ x 4¼ in.
Private collection

10 ***Flooded Cascade: Dawn Light***, 1997
Polished oil on canvas
15¾ x 8 in.
Private collection

11 ***Flooded Cascade on the Way to Robin's House***, 1999
Polished oil on canvas
72 x 36 in.
Private collection

12 ***Flooded Canyon: Yellowstone***, 1997
Polished oil on canvas
48 x 72 in.
The National Museum of American Art, Smithsonian Institution

13 ***Flooded Canyon: Yellowstone (Storm Approaching)***, 1998
Polished oil on canvas
66 x 96 in.
Private collection

14 ***Study for Painted World***, 1997
Painted inkjet print
6 x 10 in.
Private collection

15 ***Annie's Painting***, 1998
Polished oil on canvas
48 x 72 in.
Interscope Communications

16 ***Study #1: The Oxbow***, 1992
Polished oil on canvas
4¼ x 6¼ in.
Collection of the Artist

17 ***The Oxbow, After Church, After Cole, Flooded***, 1979–1994
(Flooded River for the Matriarchs: E. and A. Mongan)
Polished oil on canvas
54 x 81 in.
The Smith College Museum of Art

18 ***The Oxbow, After Church, After Cole, Flooded***, 1998
(Flooded River for Fran)
Polished oil on canvas
24 x 36 in.
The Boston Museum of Fine Arts

19 ***The Oxbow, After Church, After Cole, Flooded***, 1998 (Detail)
(Flooded River for the Matriarchs: E. and A. Mongan)
Polished oil on canvas
48 x 72 in.
Private collection

20 ***The Oxbow, After Church, After Cole, Flooded***, 1999
(Flooded River for the Matriarchs: E. and A. Mongan)
Polished oil on canvas
48 x 72 in.
Private collection

21 ***Flooded Cove: Dawn Light***, 1998
Polished oil on canvas
10¾ x 13⅜ in.
Private collection

22 ***Flooded Marsh: Ginger's Morning***,1996
Polished oil on canvas
12 x 22 in.
Worchester Art Museum

23 ***Caribbean Dawn: Storm Clearing***, 1995
Polished oil on canvas
12 x 22 in.
Private collection

24 ***New England City: Flooded River at Dusk***, 1999
Polished oil on canvas
11½ x 14¾ in.
Private collection

25 ***Flooded River: Evening Snow***, 1999
Polished oil on canvas
12½ x 10 in.
Private collection

26 ***Crisp Dawn Near Duncan's Ravine***, 1997
Polished oil on canvas
11¼ x 7¼ in.
Private collection

27 ***Flooded River: February Thaw***, 1997
Polished oil on canvas
10¼ x 13¼ in.
Private collection

28 ***Flooded Orchard at the End of the Day***, 1998
Polished oil on canvas
16¼ x 12½ in.
Private collection

29 ***Nocturne for Magritte: Warm Light***, 1995
Polished oil on canvas
21 x 17 in.
Private collection

30 ***Flooded Pasture: Evening Rain***, 1999
Polished oil on canvas
24 x 36 in.
Private collection

31 ***Flooded River: Early Storm***, 1994
Polished oil on canvas
11½ x 20 in.
Private collection

32 ***Flooded River: Approaching Fog with White Light***, 1997
Polished oil on canvas
6 x 8 in.
Private collection

33 ***Flooded River: Golden Dawn, Rose Veil***, 1997
Polished oil on canvas
40 x 72 in.
Private collection

34 ***Flooded River: Evening Rain***, 1999
Polished oil on canvas
31 x 37 in.
Private collection

35 ***Flooded River: Mauve Dawn***, 1998
Polished oil on canvas
11 x 14 in.
Private collection

36 ***Flooded River: Golden Light***, 1998
Polished oil on canvas
5 x 8¾ in.
Collection of the Artist

37 ***Flooded Pasture: Morning Light***, 1999
Polished oil on canvas
12 x 22¾ in.
Private collection

38 ***Flooded River for T.M.***, 1998
Polished oil on canvas
19½ x 51 in.
Private collection

39 ***Flooded River: Orchard below the Oxbow***, 1999 (Detail)
Polished oil on canvas
40 x 72 in.
Private collection

40 ***Flooded River above the Falls***, 1995
Polished oil on canvas
12 x 22 in.
Private collection

41 ***Flooded Canal: Evening in Provence***, 1995
Polished oil on canvas
18 x 30 in.
Private collection

42 ***Flooded River for Dante and Hallie***, 1994
Polished oil on canvas
48 x 81 in.
Gramercy Tavern, New York

43 ***Marine Nocturne: Winter Light***, 1995
Polished oil on canvas
5¼ x 7⅜ in.
Collection of the Artist

44 ***Mediterranean Nocturne with Approaching Front***, 1997 (Detail)
Polished oil on canvas
28 x 38 in.
Private collection

45 ***Squid Boats on the Gulf of Siam***, 1991
Polished oil on canvas
12 x 22 in.
Collection of the Artist

46 ***Homage to the Riverkeeper***, 1993
Polished oil on canvas
30 x 24 in.
Collection of the Artist

47 ***Mountain Nocturne with New Moon***, 1996 (Detail)
Polished oil on canvas
9 x 7 in.
Private collection

48 ***Desert City Nocturne: Evening Storm***, 1999
Polished oil on canvas
8½ x 16 in.
Private collection

49 ***Nocturne for Bischoff***, 1992
Polished oil on canvas
5 x 7½ in.
Private collection

50 ***Mediterranean Nocturne: Warm Horizon at Dawn***, 1999
Polished oil on canvas
24 x 36 in.
Private collection

51 ***Bermuda Nocturne: Morning Light***, 1995
Polished oil on canvas
5½ x 4¼ in.
Collection of the Artist

52 ***Caribbean Launch at Dawn***, 1997
Polished oil on canvas
8 x 6⅛ in.
Collection of the Artist

53 ***Cool Launch at Dawn***, 1995
Polished oil on canvas
7 x 4¾ in.
Collection of the Artist

54 ***Launch at Dawn: Warm Light***, 1995
Polished oil on canvas
6¾ x 4½ in.
Private collection

55 ***Dual Launch at Dawn***, 1995
Polished oil on canvas
12 x 18 in.
Private collection

56 ***Incendiary Nocturne: Evening Launch for George***, 1998
Polished oil on canvas
39½ x 29½ in.
Private collection

57 ***Incendiary Nocturne: Mauve Dusk (Evening Launch for George)***, 1999
Polished oil on canvas
54 x 36 in.
Private collection

58 ***Vortex at Dawn: Green Light***, 1993
Polished oil on canvas
30 x 36 in.
Private collection

59 ***Vortex at Dawn***, 1996
Polished oil on canvas
31 x 38 in.
Private collection

60 ***Study: The Raft (Phase I)***, 1995
Pastel and oil over ink
10¾ x 14 in.
Private collection

61 ***Study: The Raft (Phase II)***, 1995
Pastel and oil over ink
10¾ x 14 in.
Private collection

62 ***The Raft***, 1998
Polished oil on canvas
45 x 52 in.
Private collection